The Best

Texas Cookbook

100 Favorite Lone Star Recipes

Southern Soup Jockeys

ISBN-13: 9798391368939

DEEP
IN THE
heart
OF TEXAS

THE GREAT STATE OF TEXAS

Wanted – Texas Food!

You don't have to travel to Texas to enjoy the best food in Texas. Just browse through these 100 recipes to find new favorite foods that your family will love.

Of course, barbecue is one food you can find everywhere in Texas. Barbecue does change depending on the region of Texas, but all Texans agree their barbecue is the best!

TEXAS BARBECUE

Who doesn't love barbecue? Texas barbecue and food in general influences were Germany, Louisiana, the Czech Republic and, of course, Mexico. The Czech and German immigrants to Texas brought their traditions of smoking meat with them, resulting in the now famous Texas barbecue.

Some regions of Texas serve barbecue with little or no sauce, while others coat their brisket in barbecue sauce. Brisket is so popular in Texas that you can even order brisket breakfast tacos in some places.

TEXAS CHILI

Chili was adopted as the Texas state dish on May 11, 1977, and Texas Chili Cook-Offs are held everywhere in the state all year long.

Beans vs. No Beans - If you live in Texas, there will be no beans in your chili. But beans make the chili last longer, thus making it more cost effective. So, add beans if you must. Beans or not, it's still chili.

TEX-MEX FOOD

Tex-Mex is a relatively new cooking style. With Tex-Mex food having almost the same taste as Mexican food, sometimes it is hard to tell if you are eating Tex-Mex or authentic Mexican food. Burritos are Tex-Mex. Nachos are Mexican with a pinch of Texas. Hard shell tacos are a Tex-Mex classic as Mexican tacos are usually made from a soft tortilla.

The difference can be found in the use of ingredients – such as yellow cheese, beef, or wheat flour. If a recipe calls for any of these ingredients, it's most likely Tex-Mex food. Beef is the primary choice for Tex-Mex but is not usually used in authentic Mexican food.

So, which is better?

One main difference between traditional Mexican food and Tex-Mex is that Mexican food is lighter. Alot of Tex-Mex food is covered in yummy cheese. If the sauce is red, creamy and cheesy, the food is probably Tex-Mex.

Typically, when you are hungering for authentic Mexican food, you want cuisines that use only Mexican ingredients. On the flip side, Tex-Mex has a smaller set of base ingredients. Both authentic Mexican and Tex-Mex food have a delicious and flavorful taste – so it's your preference. There are definitely Tex-Mex recipes in this cookbook. Tex-Mex, chili and barbecue are among our favorite foods in Amarillo, Texas!

Barbecue

Barbecue Brisket Tacos

With this recipe, you can create 8 Barbecue Brisket Tacos that are bursting with flavor. These tacos are packed with smoky and savory goodness and a quick dinner option for using up leftover shredded barbecue brisket.

2 cups barbecue brisket
8 corn tortillas
Non-stick cooking spray
1/2 cup shredded cheddar cheese
1/4 cup Pico de Gallo
1/4 cup sour cream
1/4 cup fresh cilantro, chopped
2 limes, cut into 8 wedges

Using a large skillet, spray pan lightly with cooking spray and heat until hot over medium high heat. Add a tortilla and cook 1 minute per side, until lightly browned. Repeat with remaining tortillas, spraying with oil as needed.

Heat brisket until hot in microwave.

Assembly: Lay the tortillas flat. Add 1/4 cup brisket down the center of each tortilla. Add cheese, Pico de Gallo, sour cream, cilantro, and lime juice.

Yield: 8 tacos.

Hogeye's Barbecued Ham

This recipe is for a delicious and hearty ham sandwich. Chopped deli ham is cooked with onions, green peppers, butter, brown sugar, mustard, Worcestershire sauce, chili sauce, and barbecue sauce. Served hot and enjoy with pickles.

1-1/2 lb. chopped deli ham (or have it shaved paper thin at the deli)
3 teaspoons butter or margarine
1 onion, finely chopped
1 green pepper, finely chopped
4 teaspoons brown sugar
1 teaspoon prepared mustard
1 tablespoon Worcestershire sauce
1 bottle chili sauce, (12 oz.)
1-1/2 cups bottled barbecue sauce
Sandwich buns or split kaiser rolls

In a large skillet, cook onion and green pepper in butter until onion is translucent, about 5 minutes. Stir in brown sugar, mustard, Worcestershire sauce, chili sauce and barbecue sauce.

Simmer for 1 hour, then stir in ham. Cook 5 to 10 minutes more until ham is heated through.

While ham is simmering, heat the sandwich buns or rolls in a 275 degrees F. oven until toasted, about 5 minutes.

Divide ham mixture among the sandwich buns. Serve hot, with pickles.

Yield: 8 sandwiches.

Barbecued Beef Brisket

With its irresistible blend of flavors and tender melt-in-your-mouth texture, this Barbecued Beef Brisket is a true crowd-pleaser that will have everyone coming back for seconds.

1 (4- to 6-pound) beef brisket
1 cup red wine vinegar
3/4 cup brown sugar, packed
3/4 cup unsweetened pineapple juice
1/2 cup molasses
1/2 cup prepared mustard
2 tablespoons minced onion
1/4 cup Worcestershire sauce
1-1/2 teaspoons chili powder
1/4 teaspoon hot sauce

Place brisket in a resealable plastic freezer bag. In a large bowl, combine the remaining ingredients, stirring well. Split the marinade evenly into 2 bowls. Pour one bowl over brisket in bag and zip bag closed. Turn bag to coat brisket thoroughly. Place bag in refrigerator for at least 4 hours or overnight, turning bag occasionally. Keep the other bowl of marinade covered in refrigerator until time to grill.

Remove brisket from marinade, discarding marinade. Prepare fire in a covered grill. Grill brisket over medium coals until browned. Cover with lid, and grill 15 minutes. Turn brisket and baste with reserved marinade. Cover and grill brisket for an additional 15 minutes.

Wrap brisket in heavy-duty aluminum foil, allowing room for marinade. Cut a hole in top of foil; pour remaining marinade through hole over brisket. Press foil together to seal hole. Cover and continue to grill over medium coals 1-1/2 to 2 hours or until very tender. To serve, slice diagonally across grain in thin slices. Yield: 12 – 16 servings.

Here are some tips to help achieve a tender brisket:

Choose the Right Cut: Selecting a good quality brisket is crucial. Look for a well-marbled piece of meat with a thick layer of fat on one side. This fat will render during cooking and contribute to the tenderness and flavor of the brisket.

Trim Excess Fat: While the fat is essential for flavor and moisture, it's a good idea to trim any excessive or uneven fat. Leaving about ¼ inch of fat on the brisket helps protect the meat from drying out during the long cooking process.

Preheat the Grill and Cook Low and Slow: Brisket is a tough cut of meat that requires low and slow cooking to break down the collagen and connective tissues. Maintain a consistent temperature between 225-250°F (107-121°C). This slow cooking process can take several hours, depending on the brisket size.

Maintain Moisture: Place a pan of water or a water-soaked wood chunk on the grill to help maintain moisture and create a smoky environment. Spritz the brisket occasionally with water or apple cider vinegar mixture to keep it moist.

Rest and Slice: Once the internal temperature reaches around 195-205°F (90-96°C), remove the brisket from the grill and let it rest for at least 30 minutes. Beyond 210°F the brisket will begin to dry out. (More brisket tips on page 22.)

Easy Barbecued Chicken

Enjoy the yummy flavors of chicken with this simple and delicious recipe. The chicken is baked to perfection, resulting in juicy and flavorful bites.

Use 3 to 4 pounds of chicken pieces.

Sauce:

1 teaspoon chili powder
1 teaspoon dry mustard
1 teaspoon salt
1 teaspoon paprika
1 teaspoon garlic salt
1 tablespoon lemon juice
4 tablespoons water
2 tablespoons olive or vegetable oil
3 tablespoons ketchup
2 tablespoons vinegar
3 tablespoons brown sugar
2 tablespoons Worcestershire sauce

In a medium saucepan, mix all ingredients for sauce and heat slowly. Dip chicken pieces in sauce and place in a 13x9x2-inch baking dish. Pour remaining sauce over chicken pieces.

Cover baking dish with foil. Bake in a 350 degrees F. oven for 2 hours, removing foil for the last 20 minutes.

Western Style Steak

Indulge in the rustic and hearty flavors of this Western Style Steak, perfect for a comforting dinner that will transport your taste buds to the Old West.

1 1/2 lbs. round steak
Salt and pepper to taste
3 tablespoons vegetable oil
2 tablespoons all-purpose flour
1 tablespoon brown sugar
1/2 teaspoon dry mustard
1 teaspoon paprika
1/4 teaspoon chili powder
1 cup tomatoes, chopped
2 tablespoons ketchup
1 tablespoon Worcestershire sauce
1 onion, sliced
1 green pepper, sliced

In a large skillet, brown steak in 3 tablespoons vegetable oil; season with salt and pepper to taste.

Mix dry ingredients in bowl; add tomatoes, ketchup, and Worcestershire sauce gradually.

Pour sauce over steaks; add sliced onion and green pepper on top. Cover; simmer for 30 minutes. Uncover, simmer for 15 minutes longer.

Easy Baked Barbecued Spareribs

This is an easy dish that will have everyone eagerly reaching for seconds. Whether it's a casual family dinner or a backyard gathering, these Easy Baked Barbecued Spareribs are sure to be a hit. Enjoy finger-licking goodness that will leave you wanting more.

4 lbs. pork spareribs
2 onions, diced
1/2 cup ketchup
1 tablespoon Worcestershire sauce
1/8 teaspoon chili powder
1 cup water

Cut ribs into serving pieces. Place in a 13x9x2-inch baking dish.

In a medium bowl, combine onions, ketchup, Worcestershire sauce, chili powder and water. Pour over top of ribs. Cover and bake at 350 degrees F for about 2 hours. Baste ribs with sauce a few times during baking.

Beef and Bean Barbecue

With the hearty combination of beef, beans, and flavorful ingredients, Beef and Bean Barbecue is a satisfying meal that will have your taste buds craving more.

1 lb. lean ground beef
1/4 cup green pepper, chopped
1/2 cup onion, chopped
1/2 cup celery, diced
1 can tomato sauce, 15 oz.
1/2 cup water
1 clove garlic
2 tablespoons vinegar
1 teaspoon mustard
2/3 teaspoon thyme
1 tablespoon brown sugar
Salt and pepper to taste
1 can pork and beans, 28 oz.

In a large skillet, brown beef and onions. In a large bowl, combine all other ingredients except the beans. Add mixture to skillet. Simmer 45 minutes or until vegetables are cooked.

Pour beef mixture in a casserole dish, stir in beans, and bake 45 minutes at 375 degrees F.

Grilled Brisket with Panhandle Barbecue Sauce

Try this recipe that promises to impress your taste buds with the tender and flavorful beef brisket, complemented by a rich and tangy homemade Panhandle Barbecue Sauce.

1 (4- to 5-pound) beef brisket
1 tablespoon garlic salt
1-1/2 teaspoons coarsely ground black pepper
Panhandle Barbecue Sauce (recipe on opposite page)

Trim the big heavy fat off the brisket. Leave about 1/4-inch of fat on the back. Sprinkle brisket with garlic salt and black pepper. Wrap brisket in heavy-duty aluminum foil. Prepare fire in a covered grill. Place brisket on grill. Cover with lid, and open vent.

Grill over low coals for 2 hours or until very tender over indirect heat. Once the internal temperature reaches around 195-205°F (90-96°C), remove the brisket from the grill and let it rest for at least 30 minutes. (Beyond 210°F the brisket will begin to dry out.)

To serve, diagonally slice brisket across grain into thin slices. Serve with **Panhandle Barbecue Sauce**. (Recipe is on opposite page)

Yield: 12 servings.

Panhandle Barbecue Sauce

2 bottles ketchup, 13 oz. each
1 cup brown sugar, packed
1/2 cup butter or margarine
3 tablespoons lemon juice
2 tablespoons liquid smoke
2 tablespoons Worcestershire sauce

In a large saucepan, combine all ingredients. Bring to a boil. Reduce heat, and simmer sauce for 30 minutes, stirring occasionally. Yield: about 3-1/2 cups.

Grilling Tips:

Preheat the Grill and Cook Over Indirect Heat: For a tender brisket, it's best to cook it using indirect heat. Place the brisket on the cooler side of the grill, away from the direct flames. This allows for slow and gentle cooking, preventing the meat from becoming tough.

Don't Peek Too Often: Each time you open the grill, you lose heat and extend the cooking time. Limit the number of times you check on the brisket to avoid unnecessary temperature fluctuations. Use a meat thermometer to monitor the internal temperature instead.

Wrap in Foil: After a few hours of cooking, once the brisket reaches an internal temperature of around 165°F (74°C), you can wrap it in foil to help retain moisture. This technique, known as the "Texas crutch," can accelerate the cooking process and further tenderize the meat.

(More brisket tips on page 16)

Grilled Tri-Tip Roasts with Tequila Marinade

Elevate your grilling game with this sensational recipe that combines bold flavors and tender meat. This recipe features succulent beef loin tri-tip roasts marinated in a blend of lime juice, cilantro, tequila, and a medley of spices.

1/2 cup fresh lime juice
1/2 cup fresh cilantro, chopped
1/2 cup olive oil
1/3 cup soy sauce
1/4 cup tequila
7 garlic cloves, finely chopped
2 teaspoons grated lime zest
2 teaspoons cumin
2 teaspoons dried oregano
1 teaspoon black pepper
2 2-pound beef loin tri-tip roasts, trimmed

Whisk together lime juice, cilantro, olive oil, soy sauce, tequila, garlic, lime zest, cumin, oregano, and pepper in a medium bowl. Pierce the tri-tip roasts all over using a small sharp knife. Place the meat in a resealable plastic freezer bag. Pour marinade over roasts. Seal and refrigerate for at least 2 hours, or overnight, turning the bag occasionally.

Remove meat and discard the marinade. Grill meat over hot coals for 10 minutes per side or to the desired degree of doneness. Remove the roasts to a cutting board; let stand for 10 minutes before carving. Slice against the grain into thin strips. Yield: 8 servings.

Texas Fun Facts

Everything is Bigger in Texas: Texas is known for its motto "Everything is bigger in Texas," and it lives up to that reputation. It is the second-largest state in the United States both in terms of land area and population.

Lone Star State: Texas is often referred to as the "Lone Star State" because it was once an independent republic with a single star on its flag. The star symbolizes Texas as a proud and independent entity.

Oil Country: Texas has a long-standing association with the oil industry. It is one of the leading oil-producing states in the United States and has played a significant role in the nation's oil production for over a century.

State Flower: The bluebonnet is the state flower of Texas. Every spring, these vibrant blue wildflowers bloom across the state, creating picturesque landscapes and attracting tourists and locals alike.

Cultural Diversity: Texas is a melting pot of cultures and ethnicities. It has been influenced by Native American, Spanish, Mexican, German, Czech, and African American cultures, among others. This diverse heritage is reflected in its cuisine, music, and festivals.

Texas Chili

Beans or no beans in chili? If you live in Texas, NO beans! No beans in Texas-style chili unless you want to be banned from Texas. Now for you bean-lovers out there, some of the chili recipes include beans in parentheses. If you are from Texas, ignore the beans please.

Serve this thick chili in a bowl with toppings like shredded cheddar cheese, sour cream, sliced jalapeños or even Fritos. Or warm flour tortillas and add the chili and toppings; roll up like a burrito.

Original Texas Chili

4 ancho chile peppers (dried poblano peppers)
4 lbs. 80/20 ground beef chuck (or boneless beef chuck roast, trim fat, cut into 1-inch cubes)
1/8 lb. beef suet, sliced thin or a tablespoon vegetable oil
4 tablespoons chili powder
2 or 3 cloves garlic, minced
3/4 cup finely chopped onion
1 teaspoon ground cumin
1/2 teaspoon oregano
Salt to taste

Wash the ancho chiles; cut chiles in half and remove stems and seeds.

Boil ancho chiles in a little water for 30 minutes. Save the water when finished. (Remove the chile skin with the back of a knife, if desired.)

Puree chiles with a little of their cooking water in a blender. Set aside.

In a large, heavy stockpot or kettle, cook suet over medium heat until a tablespoon of fat is in the bottom of the kettle. Crumble ground beef into hot suet and stir just until beef is dark gray in color – do not brown. Or if using chuck roast, sear the meat on all sides.

Add chili powder, stir, and simmer for 5 minutes. Add garlic, onion, cumin, oregano, and salt. Stir in chile puree. Cover and simmer on low for 2 to 3 hours, stirring occasionally and adding a small amount of hot water or chicken stock, as needed. (Chili will be thick – if not thick enough, add a tablespoon or two of masa harina to thicken.)

Spicy Chili with Green Chiles

This recipe yields a generous amount of chili, perfect for feeding a crowd or for leftovers to enjoy the next day. The hearty dish, with its star ingredient of green chiles, is packed with robust flavors and a kick of heat.

3 lbs. ground beef
2 cups celery, chopped
1 large onion, chopped
1 can green chiles, chopped, 8 oz.
6 tablespoons chili powder
2 tablespoons minced garlic
1 tablespoon salt
2 tablespoons granulated sugar
2 tablespoons ground cumin
1 tablespoon coriander seeds
2 cans whole tomatoes, pureed, 28 oz. each
(1 can chili beans in sauce, 15 oz.), optional
1 cup shredded cheddar or Monterey jack cheese

Garnish:

Chopped green onions
Shredded cheese
Corn chips
Chopped lettuce

Sauté ground beef in a large saucepan until brown. Add celery and onion; cook for 5 minutes. Drain the fat from the pan and discard. Add chiles, chili powder, garlic, salt, sugar, cumin, coriander seeds, tomatoes, and optional beans. (Beans can be rinsed in a colander to remove the sauce.)

Bring the mixture to a boil, then reduce heat, and simmer for 2 1/2 hours. Add shredded cheese and cook for 30 minutes. Serve with garnishes.

Cowboy Chili

Saddle up and get ready for a bold and hearty bowl of Cowboy Chili! This recipe brings together a medley of robust spices and tender beef chuck to create a chili that captures the spirit of the rugged frontier.

1 teaspoon chicken bouillon granules
1 teaspoon jalapeño powder
1 tablespoon onion powder
3 teaspoons garlic powder
1/2 teaspoon cayenne pepper
1 1/2 teaspoons black pepper
1 tablespoon paprika
6 tablespoons chili powder
2 teaspoons ground cumin
1/2 teaspoon salt
1 package Sazon Goya seasoning
2 lbs. beef chuck tender steak
1 teaspoon vegetable oil
1 tablespoon chili powder
2 teaspoons garlic powder
1 can tomato sauce, 8 oz.
1 can beef broth, 14.5 oz. or homemade beef stock
2 cups water
2 serrano peppers

In a medium bowl, combine chicken bouillon granules, jalapeño powder, onion powder, garlic powder, cayenne pepper, black pepper, paprika, chili powder, cumin, salt and Sazon Goya seasoning.

Cut beef into 1/2" cubes. In a 3-quart saucepan, brown the beef in oil. Add 1 tablespoon chili powder and 2 teaspoons garlic powder while browning. Drain fat.

Add to the saucepan: tomato sauce, beef broth and water. Stir in seasonings mixture. Float the serrano peppers (remove peppers when they become soft.) Bring to a boil, reduce heat and simmer for 2 hours, stirring occasionally.

Kickapoo Texas Chili

Prepare yourself for a bowl of chili that embodies the spirit and boldness of Texas. With each spoonful, you'll experience the perfect balance of heat, smokiness, and savory goodness.

2 1/2 lbs. lean ground beef or ground round sirloin
1 lb. ground hot sausage roll
2 tablespoons hot chili powder
(3 cans hot chili beans Bush, 16 oz. each), optional
1 can spicy V-8 juice, 5.5 oz.
2 cans stewed tomatoes, 14.5 oz. each
32 oz. tomato juice
1 can tomato soup, 10.75 oz.
1 green pepper, chopped
1 green onion, chopped
3 or 4 jalapeño peppers chopped
Salt and black pepper to taste

Brown ground beef in a large skillet. Mix in hot chili powder while browning. When browned, drain fat, remove ground beef, and cook sausage.

In a large stockpot, add optional beans, V-8 juice, stewed tomatoes, tomato juice, tomato soup, green pepper, green onion, and jalapeno peppers.

Add beef and sausage to stockpot and cook 4 to 6 hours over low-medium heat until desired thickness. Add salt, pepper, and additional chili powder according to taste preference.

Yield: 10 to 12 servings.

On a Tortilla

Breakfast Tacos

Start your day off right with these satisfying and flavorful Breakfast Tacos. With a combination of savory turkey bacon, gooey cheese, and fluffy scrambled eggs, these tacos are a delicious way to fuel your morning.

4 slices turkey bacon
2 small flour tortillas (7-inches)
4 tablespoons Cheddar cheese, shredded
2 egg whites
1 tablespoon chopped green chiles
Salsa(optional)
Additional shredded Cheddar cheese (optional)

Over medium-high heat, cook bacon in a non-stick skillet for 8 or 9 minutes or until lightly browned. On each tortilla, place 2 turkey bacon slices, then sprinkle each with 2 tablespoons of cheese. Beat chiles with egg whites; add to hot skillet. Cook and stir for 2 minutes or until eggs are done. Split egg mixture between the 2 flour tortillas. Fold tortillas over the filling. Top with additional cheese and salsa.

Yield: 2 burritos.

Slow Cooker Chalupas

Savor the irresistible flavors of Slow Cooker Chalupas with this easy and delicious recipe. The slow cooker does all the work, allowing the flavors to meld together and the meat to become irresistibly tender.

2 lb. pork roast
1 lb. pinto beans
2 teaspoons minced garlic
1 teaspoon cumin seed
1 teaspoon oregano
4 teaspoons hot taco sauce
1 teaspoon salt
1/4 teaspoon ginger
4 cups water
Tortilla chips or flour tortillas

Spray slow cooker with cooking spray. In a bowl, combine pinto beans, garlic, cumin seed, oregano, taco sauce, salt, ginger, and water. Place pork roast in slow cooker. Pour pinto bean mixture over roast. Add water if necessary to cover roast. Make sure some liquid gets under the roast.

Cover and cook on low for 5 hours. Check after 5 hours and if liquid has been absorbed, add 1 cup of water. Cook for 3 to 4 more hours, adding water as necessary. Cook until beans are done, and roast is tender.

Remove the roast and shred the meat with 2 forks. Return meat to the slow cooker. Cook on low for 30 minutes.

***To serve**: Slightly crush tortilla chips on plates. Add chalupa mixture on top. Garnish with grated cheese, lettuce, tomatoes, olives, sour cream, etc.*

Or if using flour tortillas, warm tortillas for a few seconds in the microwave before filling with meat mixture and garnishes.

Enchilada Hot Dish

Serve this easy-to-make Enchilada Hot Dish as a main course, accompanied by your favorite sides like Mexican rice, refried beans, or a fresh green salad.

10 to 12 flour tortillas, (8-inch)
1 can chopped green chiles or jalapeño peppers, drained, 4 oz.
2 cups sour cream or plain yogurt
Ricotta, cottage cheese, or tofu, 24 oz.
1/2 teaspoon salt
1/8 teaspoon black pepper
12 slices sharp cheddar cheese
Sauce (recipe below)

Spray a 13x9x2 baking dish with non-stick cooking spray. In a medium bowl, mix chiles or peppers, sour cream or yogurt, Ricotta, salt, and pepper. Put cheddar cheese strips and chile mixture on each tortilla. Roll up and place seam side down in greased baking dish. Cover with sauce (recipe below). Bake at 350 degrees F for 25 to 30 minutes.

Yield: 6 servings.

Sauce:

2 tablespoons chopped onion
1 garlic clove, minced
1 tablespoon vegetable oil
1 to 2 teaspoons chili powder
1 tablespoon all-purpose flour
1 can diced tomatoes, 20 oz.
1/2 teaspoon salt

1/4 teaspoon Tabasco sauce

Sauté onion and garlic in oil until soft. Stir in chili powder and flour. Add tomatoes, salt and Tabasco sauce, simmer until thickened.

Mesquite Fajitas

Enjoy the flavors of the Southwest with these tantalizing Mesquite Fajitas. Marinated in a zesty blend of lime juice, garlic salt (or fresh garlic), and black pepper, the flank or skirt steak is then grilled to perfection over medium-hot mesquite coals, resulting in a charred and succulent centerpiece for your fajitas.

1 lb. flank or skirt steak, trimmed of fat
Juice of 2 to 3 limes
1 to 1-1/2 teaspoons garlic salt or 2 garlic cloves, chopped
1/2 teaspoon black pepper
4 flour tortillas, (8-inch)
2 bell peppers, seeded and cut into strips
1/2 onion, cut into strips
Toppings, if desired - chopped tomato, green onions, guacamole, sour cream, cheddar cheese, picante sauce, taco sauce

Place steak in a resealable freezer bag. Combine lime juice, garlic salt, and black pepper, stirring well; pour over steak, and secure bag tightly. Turn bag to coat steak thoroughly. Place bag in refrigerator; refrigerate 6 hours or overnight, turning bag occasionally.

Lightly oil a ridged grill pan. Preheat the grill pan on high heat. Remove steak from marinade. (Discard marinade.) Grill the steak over medium-hot mesquite coals for 5 to 6 minutes on each side or until desired degree of doneness. When the steak is off the grill pan, add some olive oil to the grill pan and add the bell peppers and onions. Grill for about 8 minutes until the onions and peppers are limp.

Wrap tortillas in aluminum foil and heat in 300 degrees F oven for 10 to 15 minutes or until thoroughly heated. Set tortillas aside and keep warm.

Diagonally slice steak across grain into thin slices. Place steak on tortillas and top with any of the following ingredients: cheddar cheese, tomato, green onions, guacamole, sour cream, picante sauce, or taco sauce.

Yield: 4 servings.

Chimichangas

Once the chimichangas are cooked to perfection, transfer them to a plate and garnish generously with mild salsa verde, shredded lettuce, diced tomatoes, grated cheddar cheese, and a dollop of sour cream.

2 lbs. chuck roast, cut into pieces
3 cups water or beef stock
1/2 cup diced green chiles
1 tablespoon black pepper
1 teaspoon salt
1 cup crushed tomatoes
8 flour tortillas (10-inch)
2 cups vegetable oil
2 cups mild salsa verde
2 cups shredded lettuce
1 large tomato, seeded and diced
2 cups grated cheddar cheese
1 cup sour cream

Brown the meat on both sides in a heavy skillet. Transfer the meat to a large Dutch oven and add water or beef stock. Cover and cook in a 325 degrees F. oven for 2 1/2 hours, or until tender. Drain, cool, and shred the meat with two forks. Place the shredded meat in a large skillet and add green chiles, pepper, salt, and tomatoes. Simmer over low heat for 30 minutes.

Divide the mixture evenly in the center of the tortillas. Roll up the mixture in the tortilla by folding the bottom up first, then each side over, then the top.

Heat the vegetable oil in a large skillet. When it is hot, place 4 chimichangas in the oil, bottom side down first and cook for 4 minutes. Repeat. Place 2 chimichangas on a plate and top with equal amounts of salsa verde, lettuce, tomatoes, cheese, and sour cream. Serve immediately.

Quesadillas Mission Style

Savor the delightful combination of melted cheeses, sautéed peppers and onions, and zesty toppings that make these quesadillas a true delight.

Feel free to add grilled and cut-up chicken, steak, shrimp, or crabmeat to the tortilla for an added protein boost and an extra layer of deliciousness.

1 green pepper, julienned
1 onion, cut in strips

8 flour tortillas, (10-inch)
Monterey Jack cheese, grated, 8 oz.
Cheddar cheese, grated, 8 oz.

1 tomato, chopped
1 can diced green chiles, 4 oz.

In a saucepan, sauté onions and peppers to desired degree of doneness.

Spread 1/4 of both the Monterey Jack and cheddar cheese over one flour tortilla, leaving 1/2-inch around the edge uncovered. Add 1/4 of the green pepper and onion mixture, a few chopped tomatoes and green chiles on top of the cheese. Top with another flour tortilla.

Spray a skillet with non-stick cooking spray. Heat the skillet over medium-high heat until hot, then add quesadilla to the skillet and lower heat to medium. Cook 1 to 2 minutes on each side until the cheese melts and bottom is golden brown and tortilla is crisp. Continue with remaining tortillas.

Place quesadillas on plates and cut them into four or five sections. Serve with sour cream, salsa, and guacamole. If you wish, add grilled, cut up chicken, steak, shrimp, or crabmeat to tortilla.

Southwest Lasagna

Combining the elements of traditional lasagna with the vibrant and zesty flair of Southwest cuisine, this dish is sure to become a family favorite.

2 lbs. ground beef
1 package taco seasoning, 1 oz.
1 cup water
1 can tomato sauce, 15 oz.
12 corn tortillas
1-1/2 cups sour cream
Cheddar cheese, shredded, 8 oz.
1/2 cup green onion, chopped

Brown ground beef in a large skillet and drain off grease. Add taco seasoning and water; simmer for 15 minutes. Add tomato sauce and simmer 5 minutes longer. If desired, lightly butter tortillas. Spread half of meat mixture in bottom of 9x13x2-inch baking pan; cover with 6 tortillas and spread with half of sour cream; repeat.

Top with cheese and chopped green onion. Bake, uncovered, 30 minutes at 350 degrees F.

Cheesy Chicken Enchiladas

Prepare to delight your taste buds with these irresistible Cheesy Chicken Enchiladas. The combination of delicious fillings, cheese, and zesty toppings makes this dish an absolute winner. Enjoy a fiesta of flavors with every bite!

1 cup sour cream, divided
4 cups shredded cheddar cheese, divided
2 cups cooked chicken, shredded
1/4 cup chopped onion
8 flour tortillas (8-inch) or corn tortillas
1/2 cup black olives, sliced
1 1/2 cups tomatoes, chopped

In a large bowl, mix 1 cup cheese, chicken, onions, and 3/4 cup sour cream.

In a medium saucepan, mix 1/4 cup sour cream and 3 cups cheese. Cook on low until cheese is melted, stirring occasionally.

Spray a 13x9x2-inch baking dish lightly with cooking spray. Warm 2 tortillas at a time in the microwave for 7 seconds. Down the center of each tortilla, spread a little less than 1/2 cup chicken mixture. Roll up each tortilla around filling and place seam side down in baking dish in a single layer. Pour sour cream and cheese mixture over tortillas, then top with black olives and tomatoes.

Bake at 350 degrees F for 20 to 25 minutes, or until bubbly.

Lone Star State Fajitas

Transport yourself to the Lone Star State with these tantalizing fajitas. Bursting with flavor and sizzling with Tex-Mex goodness, this dish captures the essence of Texas cuisine.

1 lb. sliced beef, chicken, pork, or venison
2 cloves garlic, minced
1 teaspoon cumin
1/8 teaspoon oregano
1/4 teaspoon salt
2 tablespoons lemon or lime juice
2 tablespoons vinegar
Dash of hot sauce
2 tablespoons olive oil
1 onion, peeled and sliced
1 green pepper, sliced
4 flour tortillas, (6-inch)
Salsa, sour cream, grated cheddar cheese for serving

Slice meat into 8-inch strips. In a small bowl, mix garlic, cumin, oregano, salt, lemon or lime juice, vinegar, and hot sauce. Place meat in a resealable freezer bag and pour spice mixture over meat. Place in refrigerator and marinade for 4 hours or overnight.

Discard marinade. In a heavy skillet, heat olive oil. Stir fry meat, onions, and peppers. Serve with heated tortillas, salsa, sour cream, and grated cheese.

Baked Chicken Chimichangas

4 flour tortillas (10-inch)
1-1/2 cups boiled chicken breast
Black pepper to taste
Garlic powder to taste
Grated cheddar cheese, 4 oz.
1 medium tomato, diced
1 small onion, diced
1 can diced green chiles, 4 oz.
1 can tomato puree, 29 oz.
1 cup salsa (mild, medium, or hot)

Spray a 10x10x2-inch baking dish with non-stick cooking spray.

Boil chicken. Shred chicken using two forks; season with black pepper and garlic powder to taste. Mix shredded chicken with cheese, tomato, onion and green chiles. Warm tortillas, one at a time in microwave for about 7 seconds. Spoon 1/4 to 1/3 cup chicken mixture on tortillas. Fold to hold the filling.

Lay chimichangas, seam side down, on the baking dish. Bake 15 minutes at 375 degrees F. Mix together salsa and tomato puree to use as sauce, and warm before serving. Top chimichanga with sauce, lettuce, tomatoes, cheese, and sour cream as desired.

Turkey Enchiladas

Take your taste buds on a fiesta with a delightful twist on a classic Mexican dish. Bursting with flavor and enveloped in a zesty tomato sauce, these turkey enchiladas are sure to become a new family favorite.

This recipe is perfect for utilizing leftover turkey, making it a delicious option for post-holiday meals or anytime you crave a taste of Tex-Mex.

Serve these enchiladas as a centerpiece to your Mexican-inspired feast, accompanied by your favorite sides like Mexican rice, refried beans, or chips and salsa.

10 flour tortillas (6-inch)
1 can diced tomatoes, 14.5 oz.
1 can tomato sauce, 15 oz.
1 cup finely chopped green pepper
1/2 cup sliced green onions
1/4 cup snipped parsley
1 teaspoon chili powder
1/2 teaspoon crushed red pepper
1/4 teaspoon cumin
2 cups cooked turkey, chopped
3 oz. cream cheese softened, 3 oz.
1 cup shredded cheddar cheese

Spray a 13x9x2-inch baking dish with non-stick cooking spray.

Sauce:
In a saucepan, combine undrained tomatoes, tomato sauce, green pepper, onions, parsley, chili powder, red

pepper, and cumin. Bring to a boil. Reduce heat; simmer, uncovered, for 5 minutes.

Turkey Mixture:
In a medium bowl, combine half the sauce, turkey, cream cheese and half the shredded cheese. Spoon about 1/4 cup of the turkey mixture onto each warmed-up tortilla; roll tortilla. Place tortillas, seam side down, in baking dish.

Bake, covered, in a 350 degrees F oven for 20 minutes. Pour remaining tomato sauce mixture over tortillas, sprinkle with remaining shredded cheese. Uncover and bake for 8 to 10 minutes more. Yield: 5 servings.

Sour Cream Enchiladas

This southwest recipe brings together tender roast beef, zesty green chiles, and a luscious sour cream sauce to create a flavor-packed Mexican-inspired dish.

Meat mix:

5 lbs. roast beef (best = strip loin, sirloin, tenderloin, eye of round, top round roasts. Note: not chuck roasts)
3 onions, chopped
1 can diced green chiles, 4 oz.
3 teaspoons butter

1 teaspoon ground cumin
1/4 teaspoon garlic powder
2 cans salsa verde, 7 oz. each
4 teaspoons all-purpose flour
4 teaspoons salt
Juice from roast

Sour cream sauce:

1 can enchilada sauce, 10 oz.
1 can diced tomatoes, 14.5 oz.
1-1/2 cups cheddar cheese, shredded
1-1/2 cups sour cream

20 corn tortillas, (8-inch)
1 cup of canola oil
1 cup cheddar cheese, shredded

Beef: Cook roast beef at 200 degrees F in a roaster with lid (no salt or water) for 10 to 12 hours. Cool and shred.

Spray a 13x9x2-inch baking dish with non-stick cooking spray. In a medium bowl, combine cumin, garlic powder, salsa verde, flour, salt, and juice from roast.

In a large skillet, sauté onions and green chiles in butter. Add spice mixture from bowl. Reduce heat to low, simmer for 10 minutes, stirring often. Remove from heat and add to meat.

Sour Cream Sauce:
In a saucepan, combine enchilada sauce and tomatoes on medium heat. Cook until boiling. Lower heat to simmer and add cheese and sour cream. Simmer for 10 minutes, stirring often, just until cheese is melted. Remove from heat.

In a small skillet over medium heat, heat 1/2 cup canola oil. Fry corn tortillas one at a time just until soft. Drain on paper towels. Continue with all tortillas.

Spread 1/4 to 1/2 cup of sauce on the bottom of the baking dish. Place about 1/2 cup of sauce on a plate and dip each tortilla in the sauce. Put the soft, dipped tortilla on a plate and fill with 1/4 cup meat mixture and 2 tablespoons cheese. Roll up tight; put the overlapping seam down in baking dish. Pour sauce over tortillas and sprinkle remaining cheese on top. Bake at 350 degrees F for 30 minutes or until the cheese is melted.

Main Dishes

Slow Cooker Floating Tacos

1 lb. lean ground beef
1/2 cup onion, chopped
1 can chili with beans, 15 oz.
1 can tomato sauce, 8 oz.
1 can enchilada sauce, 10 oz.
1/2 jar picante sauce, 16 oz.
1/4 teaspoon chili powder
1/2 teaspoon garlic powder
1/2 teaspoon salt
1/4 teaspoon black pepper
Tortilla chips
Cheddar cheese
Lettuce
Sour cream

In a large skillet, brown ground beef and onion, drain. Mix browned ground beef with chili, tomato sauce, enchilada sauce, picante sauce, chili powder, garlic powder, salt, and pepper.

Cook all day in a slow cooker on low heat. To serve, layer chips, meat sauce, cheese, lettuce, sour cream, and any other taco ingredient you like.

Texas Mixed Casserole

Bursting with flavors and textures, this casserole combines a variety of ingredients to create a hearty and satisfying dish that will leave you craving for more.

1/2 cup butter or margarine, melted
1/2 cup onion, diced
3 or 4 jalapeño peppers, minced
1 egg, beaten
1 can whole kernel corn,15.25 oz., drained
1 can cream-style corn, 14.75 oz.
1 cup sour cream

1 or 2 zucchini, sliced
3 or 4 yellow squash, sliced
1/2 cup mayonnaise
1 package corn muffin mix, 8.5 oz.
1 package shredded cheddar cheese, 8 oz.

1/2 to 1 cup bread crumbs
Salt and pepper to taste

Spray a 13x9x2-inch baking dish with non-stick cooking spray. Add melted butter, onion, peppers, egg, corn, cream-style corn, and sour cream and mix well. Add zucchini and yellow squash and mix. Add mayonnaise, corn muffin mix, and cheese, stir until well combined.

Sprinkle the bread crumbs over the top and season with salt and pepper. Bake at 350 degrees F for 35 to 40 minutes.

Yield: 15 to 20 servings.

Corn Meal Chicken Pie

This delightful recipe features a homemade cornmeal crust filled with a savory chicken and vegetable mixture, topped with a golden breadcrumb topping. Serve this Corn Meal Chicken Pie as a delicious main course for any gathering or as a comforting family meal.

Crust:

1-1/4 cups all-purpose flour
3/4 cup corn meal
1 teaspoon baking powder
1/4 teaspoon baking soda
3/4 teaspoon salt
1/2 cup butter or margarine
1/2 cup sour cream

Blend flour, corn meal, baking powder, baking soda, salt, butter or margarine and sour cream in a food processor. Press in a 12-inch pie dish. Bake at 375 degrees F for 15 minutes. Prepare filling and spread over baked crust. Sprinkle topping over filling. Bake another 15 to 20 minutes at 375 degrees F or until brown.

Filling – Corn Meal Chicken Pie

1/4 cup celery, finely chopped
1/4 cup tomato, chopped
1 can cream of chicken soup, 10.5 oz.
2 cups cooked chicken, cubed
1/4 cup mushrooms, chopped
1/2 cup whole kernel corn, drained

Mix celery, tomato, soup, chicken, mushrooms, and corn. Spoon filling into prepared crust.

Topping – Corn Meal Chicken Pie

1-1/2 cups dry bread crumbs
1/4 teaspoon poultry seasoning
1/8 teaspoon salt
1/8 teaspoon black pepper
1 teaspoon onion, finely chopped
2 teaspoons melted butter
2 teaspoons hot water

Mix dry bread crumbs, poultry seasoning, salt, pepper, onion, butter, and hot water together. Sprinkle on top of pie.

Chipotle Pork Tenderloin

Experience a burst of smoky and spicy flavors with this tasty Chipotle Pork Tenderloin recipe. Tender pork tenderloin is marinated in a flavorful blend of herbs and spices, then grilled to perfection before being baked in a tangy and sweet chipotle sauce.

1 2-lb. pork tenderloin, trimmed
1 cup olive oil
1 tablespoon oregano
1 tablespoon thyme
2 tablespoons garlic powder, divided
Salt and black pepper to taste
1 cup soy sauce
1 cup ketchup
1 tablespoon curry powder
1 jar chipotle salsa, 7 oz.
1 cup brown sugar, packed
1/2 cup balsamic vinegar

Place the meat in a sealable freezer bag. Combine olive oil, oregano, thyme, 1 tablespoon garlic powder, salt and pepper in a small bowl and mix well. Pour the marinade over the meat. Seal and refrigerate for 8 hours, turning occasionally.

Remove the tenderloin, discarding the marinade. Grill the tenderloin, covered with grill lid, over high heat for 3 minutes. Turn and cook for 3 minutes longer.

Place meat in a 13x9x2-inch baking dish. In a medium bowl, combine soy sauce, ketchup, 1 tablespoon garlic powder, curry powder, salsa, brown sugar, and vinegar and mix well. Pour the sauce over meat, reserving 3/4 cup of the sauce.

Bake at 350 degrees F for 30 to 45 minutes or to 160 degrees F on a meat thermometer. Serve with the heated reserved sauce. Yield: 8 servings.

Chicken Fajita Baked Potatoes

Chicken Fajita Baked Potatoes are a fantastic meal that combines the comfort of a baked potato with the bold flavors of fajitas. Perfectly baked potatoes are loaded with a perfect combination of sautéed bell peppers, onions, seasoned chicken, cheese, and tangy salsa.

4 large baking potatoes
1 medium red or green bell pepper, cut into strips
1/4 cup chopped onion
1 tablespoon margarine or butter
1 envelope fajita seasoning mix, 1 oz.
1 can sliced black olives drained, 2.25 oz.
Cooked chicken breasts, cut into strips, 6 oz.
1/2 cup shredded cheddar cheese, 2 oz.
2 tablespoons diced canned green chiles
1 cup salsa
Sour cream
Guacamole

Scrub the potatoes and pat dry. Prick potatoes with a fork and arrange potatoes on a microwave-safe pie plate. Microwave on High for 15 to 18 minutes or until the potatoes are tender, turning the pie plate 2 times and turning potatoes over once.

Sauté bell pepper and onion in margarine or butter in a saucepan over medium heat until tender. Add fajita seasoning mix and sauté for 1 minute longer. Remove from heat. Add olives, chicken, cheese and chiles; mix well. Cut a slit in each potato from end to end and squeeze to open the slit.

Divide chicken mixture among the potatoes. Spoon 1/4 cup salsa on top of the chicken mixture on each potato. Microwave for 5 minutes or until heated through. Garnish potatoes with dollops of sour cream, guacamole, and additional salsa.

Yield: 4 servings.

Smokie Meat Balls

These meatballs are bursting with flavor and make a fantastic appetizer or main dish. Serve them on a platter with toothpicks for easy snacking or pair them with pasta or rice for a satisfying meal.

2 lbs. ground beef
1/2 teaspoon black pepper
1 teaspoon garlic powder
1 teaspoon salt
3 egg yolks
3 egg whites, stiffly beaten
1/2 cup milk
3 slices bread, soaked in water and wrung out
1 medium onion, chopped

In a large bowl, mix ground beef, pepper, garlic powder, salt, egg yolks only, milk, bread, and onion until just combined. Fold in stiffly beaten egg whites.

Use about one tablespoon of meat per meatball and form into small balls. (Lightly oiled hands will prevent meat from sticking to your hands.)

Line a baking sheet with parchment paper and lightly spray parchment paper with non-stick cooking spray. Add meatballs to baking sheet.

Bake at 350 degrees F for approximately 30 minutes.

Sauce:

1 can crushed tomatoes, 28 oz.

2 tablespoons tomato paste
2 tablespoons liquid smoke
1 tablespoon fresh parsley or basil, chopped
4 teaspoons Worcestershire sauce
1 teaspoon Italian seasoning
1 teaspoon sugar
1/2 teaspoon salt
1/2 teaspoon red pepper
1/8 teaspoon garlic powder

Mix all sauce ingredients in a medium saucepan. Simmer over medium heat for about 10 minutes, stirring occasionally. Add baked meatballs to the sauce. Stir to coat and simmer for about 3 minutes or until warm.

Chicken Delight (Overnight Casserole)

Delight your taste buds with this scrumptious recipe. This comforting dish is perfect for busy households, as it can be prepared in advance and baked to perfection the next day.

1 cup chicken broth
1/4 cup butter or margarine, melted
1 package stuffing mix, 6 oz.
3 cups cooked chicken, chopped
1 cup celery, finely chopped
1 cup onions, finely chopped
1/2 cup mayonnaise
2 eggs slightly beaten
1-1/2 cups milk
1 can cream of chicken soup, 10.5 oz.
1 cup shredded cheddar cheese

In a large bowl, add chicken broth and butter to the stuffing mix.

Put half of the stuffing mix in a well-greased, 13x9x2-inch baking dish.

Mix chicken, celery, and onion. Add mayonnaise and put this mixture on top of dressing in baking dish. Add the other half of dressing on top of chicken mixture in dish.

Beat eggs and milk. Add chicken soup and cheese. Pour over dressing and refrigerate overnight. Bake at 350 degrees F for 40 to 50 minutes or until hot. Yield: 12 servings.

Chili Baked Fresh Perch

This dish is a perfect way to highlight the delicate and flaky nature of perch fillets and the chili sauce adds a tangy and slightly spicy kick to the dish.

2 lbs. perch fillets (can substitute tilapia or cod fillets)
3/4 cup chili sauce
1/4 cup red wine vinegar or red wine
2 tablespoons finely chopped onion
3/4 cup grated American cheese

Arrange fish in buttered, shallow baking dish. In a medium bowl, combine chili sauce, wine vinegar or red wine and onion. Spread mixture on fish and sprinkle with cheese.

Bake at 450 degrees F for 15 to 20 minutes, until fish flakes easily when tested with fork.

Yield: 4 to 6 servings.

Chicken Fried Steak

Get ready to cook a classic Southern favorite with this recipe for Chicken Fried Steak. Tender cube steaks are coated in a crispy breading and fried to perfection, resulting in a delightful dish.

4 cube steaks
2 eggs
1 cup milk
1/8 teaspoon salt
1/8 teaspoon black pepper
2 cups all-purpose flour
1 cup canola or vegetable oil

To begin, gather your ingredients and set up your workstation:
1 - In a wide bowl, whisk together eggs and milk.
2 - In a separate bowl, combine flour, salt, and pepper.
3 - Have an empty plate to receive the breaded steak.

Using one cube steak at a time, first sprinkle both sides with salt and pepper. Put about 1/2 cup of the flour mixture on a large plate. Place the steak in flour mixture, coating both sides. Then dip meat in egg mixture, turning to coat, then in flour again, turning to coat both sides. Place on clean plate and repeat with the remaining steak.

In a large skillet, heat oil over medium heat until very hot. Cook 2 cube steaks at a time in hot oil until edges are golden brown, about 3 to 5 minutes per side, flipping steak at least once. Move chicken fried steak to a paper towel lined plate, cover with foil and cook the other 2 steaks. Serve with **Country Gravy** (recipe on opposite page) and mashed potatoes.

Country Gravy

3 tablespoons margarine or butter
3 tablespoons all-purpose flour
2 cups milk, 2% or whole
1/2 teaspoon salt
1/2 teaspoon black pepper

In a small saucepan, over medium heat, melt margarine or butter then add flour. Whisk together. Cook for 2 or 3 minutes. Whisk in milk, continuously whisking until it has reached a smooth and uniform consistency. Gravy will begin to thicken. Add salt and pepper.

Honey Baked Chicken

This Honey Baked Chicken recipe is a perfect choice for a family dinner or a special occasion. Tender pieces of chicken are coated in a sweet and tangy glaze, resulting in a dish that is irresistibly delicious.

1 3 lb. fryer cut up (remove skin if desired)
1/3 cup honey
1/3 cup margarine, melted
2 tablespoons prepared mustard
1 teaspoon curry powder
1 teaspoon salt

Arrange chicken in a shallow baking pan. Combine remaining ingredients and pour over.

Bake 1-1/4 hours at 350 degrees F., basting every 15 minutes, until chicken is tender and browned.

Western Hash

Transport yourself to the flavorful tastes of the Wild West with this hearty and comforting dish - Western Hash. Made with ground beef, vegetables, diced tomatoes, and seasoned with a hint of chili powder, this recipe is sure to become a family favorite.

1 lb. ground beef
1 large onion, chopped
1 large green pepper, chopped
1 can diced tomatoes, 28 oz.
1 cup uncooked white rice
1 to 2 teaspoons chili powder
2 teaspoons salt
1/8 teaspoon black pepper

In a large skillet, lightly brown ground beef. Add onions and green pepper. Cook and stir until the onion is tender. Stir in tomatoes with liquid, rice, chili powder, salt and pepper. Cover and simmer on medium-low heat for 25 minutes or until liquid is nearly gone, stirring occasionally.

Yield: 4 to 6 servings.

El Paso Burgers

Embrace the bold and festive flavors of the Southwest with this irresistible twist on a classic burger. Made with lean ground beef, vegetables, zesty taco seasoning, and topped with a creamy and tangy combination of sour cream and salsa, these burgers are a fiesta of flavors.

2 lbs. lean ground beef
1 medium onion, finely chopped
1 small green pepper, finely chopped
1 package taco seasoning mix, 1.25 oz.
8 slices of any hot pepper cheese (pepper jack, jalapeño & habanero jack, etc.)
1/2 cup sour cream
1/2 cup salsa
8 hamburger buns

In a large bowl, combine ground beef, onion, green pepper, and taco seasoning mix; mix well. Divide meat into 8 equal pieces and form into patties. Grill or fry to desired doneness.

Top with a slice of cheese, sour cream, and salsa. Serve immediately on hamburger buns.

Vegetarian Burritos

These Vegetarian Burritos are not only visually appealing with their colorful array of ingredients but also incredibly tasty and nutritious.

6 flour tortillas, (10-inch)
1/2 cup uncooked brown or white rice
1 can black beans, drained and rinsed, 15 oz.
1/4 cup cooked corn
1 red bell pepper, thinly sliced
1 tomato, diced
1/2 cup scallions, greens only
2 tablespoons cilantro leaves only, chopped
1/4 teaspoon cumin
1/4 teaspoon salt
1/4 teaspoon black pepper
1 cup cheddar cheese, grated
1-1/2 cups shredded lettuce
1/2 cup salsa

Cook rice according to package directions.

Wrap tortillas in aluminum foil. Place in oven on warm (or 200 degrees F.) while preparing the mixture for the burritos.

In a large bowl, combine cooked rice, beans, corn, sliced pepper, diced tomatoes, sliced scallions, chopped cilantro, cumin, salt, and pepper. Mix well to combine. Divide bean mixture evenly among the warm tortillas. Top each with cheese, lettuce, and salsa.

Yield: 6 servings.

Upside Down Pizza

If you're in the mood for a unique twist on traditional pizza, then this Upside Down Pizza recipe is just what you need. With its layers of savory ingredients and a surprising crescent roll crust, this dish is guaranteed to be a hit.

1 lb. lean ground beef
1 small onion, chopped
1/2 bell pepper, chopped
1 jar pizza sauce, 24 oz.
1 tub sour cream, 8 oz.
2 bags pizza blend shredded cheese, 8 oz. each
1 package pepperoni, 6 oz.
1 refrigerated 8 ct. crescent rolls

In a large skillet, brown ground beef, onion, and bell pepper. Drain. Mix in pasta sauce. Put in bottom of 13x9x2-inch casserole dish.

Layer sour cream on top of beef mixture. Layer 1/2 of shredded cheese, then pepperoni, then rest of cheese. For the crust, take a can of refrigerated crescent rolls and flatten them out. Place the flattened crescent rolls on top of the cheese layer, creating a crust-like covering for the pizza.

Bake at 350 degrees F for 15 to 20 minutes or until the top is golden brown.

Chicken Chilaquiles

This recipe for Chicken Chilaquiles combines the irresistible flavors of tortilla chips, shredded chicken, salsa, and creamy cheese to create a meal that will delight your taste buds.

1 bag tortilla chips, 13 oz.
1 can chicken broth, 14 oz.
1 medium whole chicken, cooked and cooled
4 cups tomato salsa (red) or tomatillo salsa (green)
1 cup cream or half and half
1 bag shredded Mexican cheese blend, 8 oz.
1 to 3 medium jalapeño peppers

Lightly spray a 13x9x2-inch baking dish with non-stick cooking spray. Crush enough chips on the bottom to form approximately 1/2-inch layer. Pour 1/2 of the chicken broth over the chips.

Shred cooled chicken and place over chips. Pour enough salsa over the chicken to make sure it is covered. Pour the remaining chicken broth over salsa. Place remaining chips on top. Pour cream or half and half over top layer of chips, just to moisten. Sprinkle shredded cheese over the top. Garnish with sliced jalapeño peppers.

Bake at 350 degrees F. for approximately 30 minutes, until bubbly.

Breakfast Chilaquiles

If you're looking for a flavorful and satisfying breakfast to start your day, look no further than Breakfast Chilaquiles. This traditional Mexican dish combines crispy fried tortillas, savory eggs, zesty salsa, and melted cheese to create a delicious and hearty morning meal.

6 corn tortillas
1/3 cup canola oil or corn oil
4 eggs
1 cup tomato salsa or salsa verde
1/2 cup cheddar cheese, shredded

Cut corn tortillas into quarters (triangles). In a large skillet, heat canola oil or corn oil on medium high heat and fry the tortilla triangles. Fry on each side until crisp and golden brown; dry on paper towels.

Remove all tortillas from skillet (wipe pan clean if necessary) and crack eggs into skillet. Cook until eggs are sunny side up – do not flip eggs. (Yolks will be runny, whites are cooked). Remove eggs from skillet.

Add salsa to the skillet, cook over medium heat until thickened. Add the fried tortilla triangles, gently stir to coat with salsa. Top salsa and tortillas with cheese, then with fried eggs. Cook for a couple more minutes without stirring. Remove from heat and serve.

Texas Haystack

1 lb. lean ground beef
1 large white onion, chopped
1 package taco seasoning, 1 oz.
1 can kidney beans, rinsed and drained, 15 oz.
1 can black beans, rinsed and drained, 15 oz.
1 cup frozen corn
1 can sliced black olives, 6.5 oz.
2 jars sliced pimentos, 4 oz. each
1 bunch green onions, chopped

3 tomatoes, chopped
1 package shredded Mexican mixed cheeses, 32 oz.
1 package Fritos chips, 9.25 oz.
4 cups shredded lettuce
1 container guacamole, 16 oz.
1 container sour cream, 16 oz.
1 jar salsa, 16 oz.

In a large skillet, brown ground beef and onion, drain. Add taco seasoning, kidney beans, black beans, corn, and sliced olives. Cook over medium heat for about 10 minutes or until heated through.

Just before putting meat mixture in a serving dish, add pimentos and green onions, mix well. On the side, serve tomatoes, cheese, chips, lettuce, guacamole, sour cream and salsa.

Begin building the haystack by placing the Fritos chips on a plate, top with meat mixture, lettuce, tomato, cheese and top with guacamole, salsa and sour cream.

Tex-Mex Pork Chops

If you're looking for a flavor-packed and easy-to-make dinner option, look no further than Tex-Mex Pork Chops. These tender and juicy pork chops are smothered in a savory and zesty salsa mixture, creating a delicious Tex-Mex twist on a classic dish.

4 pork chops
1 teaspoon vegetable oil
1-1/2 cups chunky salsa
1 can diced green chiles, 4 oz.
1/2 teaspoon ground cumin
1/4 cup grated cheddar cheese

In a large skillet, brown pork chops on one side in oil over medium heat, about 2 minutes. Turn pork chops. Add salsa, chiles and cumin to skillet and mix well.

Reduce heat, cover, and simmer for about 6 minutes or until cooked all the way through. (Make sure there are no pink juices.) Uncover and top each chop with 1 tablespoon cheese.

Cover and simmer until cheese melts; serve immediately.

Easy Chicken Jalapeño

Enjoy the delicious combination of tender chicken and spicy jalapeño jelly glaze. This recipe is a great way to add some excitement to your chicken dinners and satisfy your craving for a little heat.

4 skinless, boneless chicken breast halves
2 tablespoons butter or margarine, melted
1/2 cup jalapeño jelly

Place chicken breasts between two sheets of waxed paper or plastic wrap, or in a resealable plastic bag. Flatten chicken breasts to 1/4-inch thickness, using a rolling pin or the flat side of a meat mallet. Start in the center of the chicken, and work out to the edges, pounding lightly so chicken is even in thickness.

Cook chicken in butter or margarine in a large skillet over medium-high heat for 5 minutes on each side. Remove to a serving platter and keep warm. Add jelly to pan drippings; bring to a boil, stirring until smooth.

Once the glaze is ready, spoon it over the cooked chicken breasts, ensuring each piece is generously coated. The glaze adds a burst of flavor and heat, complementing the juicy chicken perfectly.

Yield: 4 servings.

Breaded Beef Short Ribs

Sink your teeth into a delight with this recipe for short ribs. These succulent and tender ribs are coated in a crispy and flavorful breading. Serve them alongside your favorite side dishes, such as mashed potatoes, steamed vegetables, or a fresh salad.

3 lbs. beef short ribs
3 tablespoons mustard
1 egg
1 teaspoon salt
4 drops tabasco sauce
2 tablespoons water
1 1/2 cups dry bread crumbs

Spread mustard over beef ribs. In a small bowl, combine egg, salt, tabasco sauce and water. Place bread crumbs in a separate bowl. Dip ribs into egg, then bread crumbs. Place on a baking sheet.

Bake at 350 degrees F for 30 min.

Yield: 4 servings.

Beans and Cornbread

Broccoli Cornbread

Add a delicious twist to traditional cornbread with this recipe for Broccoli Cornbread. Packed with a delightful combination of ingredients, this dish is a wonderful way to incorporate nutritious vegetables into a classic comfort food.

1 package frozen broccoli, thawed and drained, 10 oz.
1 medium onion, finely chopped
1/2 cup margarine or butter, melted
1 carton cottage cheese, 8 oz.
3 eggs, beaten
1 box cornbread mix, 8.5 oz.
1 teaspoon jalapeño pepper, finely chopped
3/4 teaspoon salt

In a large bowl, combine all ingredients. Pour into a greased (or spray with nonstick spray) 13x9x2-inch glass baking dish.

Bake at 350 degrees F. for 45 minutes. When done, the edges of the cornbread will turn golden brown, and the center will be moist and fluffy.

Cowboy Pinto Beans

If you're in the mood for a hearty and rustic dish that pays homage to the Old West, try this Cowboy Pinto Beans recipe. This recipe combines the rich flavors of pinto beans, smoky ham hock or salt pork, and a blend of spices to create a satisfying and comforting meal.

1 lb. dry pinto beans
1 lb. smoked ham hock or salt pork**
1 red or white onion, chopped
2 tablespoons granulated sugar
1 large bay leaf
1 teaspoon garlic powder or 6 fresh garlic cloves
1 can roasted diced green chiles, 4 oz.
1 can tomato paste, 3 oz. (optional)

Rinse the pinto beans in a colander. Pick any gravel out of the beans. Soaking the beans overnight in a large bowl filled with water will help to soften the beans and reduce the cooking time.

Alternatively, you can opt for a quick soak method by boiling a pot of water, removing it from the heat, and adding the beans. Allow the beans to soak for at least an hour before proceeding with the recipe.

To Cook: Place beans in a large pot and cover with water; add the smoked ham hock or salt pork, chopped onions, granulated sugar, bay leaf, garlic powder, green chiles, and tomato paste. Bring to a boil, then simmer over low heat (to medium-low) until done, about 1-1/2 hours to 3 hours, adding more water as needed. Cooking time will depend on how you like your beans, soft or firm.

When ham hocks are tender and falling apart, remove and let cool. Remove the meat from the ham hocks, discard bones and fat and return the meat to the beans.

Sample the beans while cooking and add salt to taste. Serve with a side of freshly baked cornbread.

**Can substitute smoked turkey necks, wings, or legs for the ham hock. Also, country ham, salt pork or bacon.

Old-Fashioned Flourless Cornbread

This cornbread recipe combines simple ingredients and classic techniques to create a deliciously moist and flavorful cornbread.

Combine in a large bowl:
2 cups yellow corn meal
1 tablespoon baking powder
1/4 teaspoon salt

Combine in smaller bowl:
1-1/4 cups plus 2 tablespoons buttermilk
1/4 teaspoon baking soda
1 tablespoon maple syrup

Whisk together and add to buttermilk mixture:
1 large egg
1 tablespoon granulated sugar
1 tablespoon corn oil

3 or 4 tablespoons butter, room temperature

Preheat oven to 375 degrees F. Preheat glass pie plate or cast-iron skillet. Add 3 or 4 tablespoons butter to hot pan (butter should be at room temperature). Combine dry and wet ingredients. Mix just until combined.

Pour batter into hot pan. Immediately place in oven. Bake at 375 degrees F. for about 25 minutes until golden brown. Cut into wedges and serve warm.

Serves 12 to 16.

Red Beans and Rice

Experience the comforting flavors of the South with this hearty recipe for Red Beans and Rice, using a combination of tender beans, smoked ham hocks, and turkey sausage.

6 cups water
1 lb. dried red kidney beans or pinto beans
3 smoked ham hocks
1/2 lb. smoked turkey sausage
2 teaspoons garlic, finely chopped
1 teaspoon salt
2 teaspoons black pepper
1/2 cup scallions including 3 inches of green tops, finely chopped
1 medium white onion, finely chopped
6 cups cooked long-grain rice

In a 3 to 4-quart saucepan, boil water over high heat. Drop in beans and boil, uncovered, for 2 minutes. Turn off heat and let beans soak for an hour. Drain beans, saving the liquid (need four cups of liquid, add water if necessary). In a crockpot, add beans and their liquid, ham hocks and sausage, garlic, salt and pepper, scallions, and onion.

Cook on high about 3 hours or until beans are very soft. Stir the pot frequently during last 30 minutes of cooking and mash some beans against the side to form a thick sauce.

Remove the ham hocks from the pot and cut off the meat. Add the meat back to the pot. Serve over hot rice.

Cornbread Dressing

Enjoy the comforting flavors of a classic Southern dish with this irresistible recipe for Cornbread Dressing. With each bite, you'll savor the rich flavors that have made this dish a favorite for generations.

3 cups cornbread, crumbled
2 tablespoons margarine or butter
1/2 cup celery, chopped
1/2 medium onion, diced
2 eggs, beaten
2 cups chicken broth
1/8 teaspoon salt
1/8 teaspoon black pepper
1 tablespoon dried sage

In a large saucepan or skillet over medium heat, melt margarine or butter. Add celery and onion; sauté for 5 minutes or until soft.

In a large bowl, put crumbled cornbread. Add onion and celery. Stir in eggs, chicken broth, salt, pepper, and sage until well combined. Should be moist. If more juice is needed, melt butter, and add a little water and onion salt to butter.

Spray a 11x7x2-inch baking dish with non-stick cooking spray and add the dressing. Bake at 350 degrees F for about 30 minutes. Bake dressing just until golden brown around edges. Be careful not to overbake as the dressing will dry out.

Santa Fe Cornbread and Cheese Squares

Savor the bold flavors and textures of these Santa Fe Cornbread and Cheese Squares. If you are craving a delicious twist on classic cornbread, these Santa Fe-inspired squares are a tasty choice.

2 packages cornbread mix, 8 oz. each
1 teaspoon salt
1 cup chopped green onions
1/2 cup chopped fresh cilantro
3 tablespoons chopped jalapeño peppers
1 cup sour cream
3/4 cup melted butter or margarine
4 eggs, beaten
1 package frozen corn with red and green peppers, thawed, drained, 16 oz.
1 cup shredded cheddar cheese

Combine both cornbread mixes, salt, green onions, cilantro, and jalapeños in a bowl. Add sour cream, butter or margarine and eggs; mix well. Add corn and cheese and mix.

Spread in a greased 13x9x2-inch baking dish. Bake at 400 degrees F for 34 to 42 minutes or until golden brown. Let stand for 10 minutes. Cut into squares.

Yield: 12 servings.

Spicy Sausage and Bean Soup

Warm up your taste buds with a bowl of comforting and flavor-packed Spicy Sausage and Bean Soup. This hearty soup combines the robust flavors of hot sausage, garlic, onion, white beans, and zesty diced tomatoes.

1 teaspoon olive oil
1 lb. bulk hot sausage
2 garlic cloves, minced
1 small onion, chopped
4 cans great northern beans undrained, 15.5 oz. each
2 cans chicken broth, 14.5 oz. each
1 can diced tomatoes, undrained, 14.5 oz.
1 teaspoon black pepper

In a large soup pot, heat olive oil over medium-high heat. Add sausage, garlic, and onion; cook for about 6 minutes, stirring frequently to break up sausage, until no pink remains in the sausage.

Add beans with juice, chicken broth, tomatoes, and pepper; bring to a boil. Reduce heat to medium-low and simmer, uncovered, for 30 minutes.

Barbecue Bean Bake

This delicious dish brings together bacon, barbecue sauce, and a medley of beans for a satisfying meal.

1 lb. ground beef chuck or round
1 onion, chopped
1 lb. bacon, chopped
1/2 cup ketchup
1/2 cup barbecue sauce
1 teaspoon salt
4 tablespoons prepared yellow mustard
4 tablespoons molasses or brown sugar
1 teaspoon chili powder
3/4 teaspoon black pepper
2 cans red kidney beans, 15.5 oz. each, drained
2 cans pork and beans, 15 oz. each, drained
2 cans butter beans, 16 oz. each, drained

Brown beef, onions, and bacon. Drain off excess fat.

In a medium bowl, mix ketchup, barbecue sauce, salt, mustard, molasses or brown sugar, chili powder and pepper. Add meat mixture, kidney beans, pork and beans and butter beans. Mix well.

Combine and add all other ingredients except beans. Stir well. Add beans and combine thoroughly.

Pour into a 2-quart glass baking dish and spread evenly. Cover loosely with aluminum foil. Bake for one hour at 350 degrees F., removing foil for the last 15 minutes. Yield: 20 to 24 servings.

Dips And Appetizers

Texas Caviar

This zesty dip is a delicious blend of black-eyed peas, hominy, fresh vegetables, and a tangy Italian salad dressing. Perfect for parties or a tasty snack.

2 cans black-eyed peas drained, 15 oz. each
1 can white hominy drained, 15.5 oz.
2 medium tomatoes, chopped
4 green onions, chopped
2 cloves of garlic, minced
1 medium green pepper, chopped
1 jalapeño pepper, chopped
1/2 cup onion, chopped
1/2 cup parsley, chopped
Italian salad dressing, 8 oz.

Combine black-eyed peas, hominy, tomatoes, green onions, garlic, green pepper, jalapeño pepper, onion, and parsley in a large bowl; mix well.

Pour the salad dressing over the mixture. Marinate, covered, in the refrigerator for 2 hours or overnight. Before serving, drain a little of the excess marinade; serve with chips. Yield: 6 1/2 cups.

Fried Dill Pickles

With a simple coating and a quick fry, you'll have a delicious snack that's sure to be a hit.

3 cups Italian seasoned bread crumbs
1/2 teaspoon salt
1 teaspoon black pepper
1 teaspoon garlic powder
1/2 teaspoon cayenne pepper
1 cup of whole milk
1 egg
16 dill pickle spears or 4 dill pickles, quartered lengthwise
2 cups vegetable oil for frying

In a medium mixing bowl, mix Italian bread crumbs, salt, black pepper, garlic powder & cayenne pepper and set aside.

In a separate bowl, whisk together milk and egg. Dip pickle spears (one at a time) into milk & egg mixture, then into breadcrumb mixture; do this twice for a double coating.

Place coated pickle spears on a baking sheet, then place in freezer for approximately 30 minutes to set coating.

In a deep fryer or a large saucepan, heat cooking oil to 350 degrees F. Place pickles into heated oil and let cook until they are a light golden brown in color, 3 to 4 minutes.

Let pickles drain by placing them on a double layer of paper towels on a serving plate.

Texas' Best Queso

Using freshly grated cheese will result in a creamier queso. Pre-shredded cheese contains additives to keep the cheese from turning into a clump in the bag. That also means the cheese doesn't melt together as well when cooking.

2 tablespoons butter
2 jalapeño peppers, seeded and chopped
3 cloves garlic, minced
1/2 cup onion, chopped
1 cup cherry tomatoes, halved
2 tablespoons corn starch
1 can evaporated milk, 12 oz.
3/4 cup water
1/2 lb. American cheese white, grated
1/2 lb. American cheese yellow, grated
1 can fire roasted chopped green chiles, 4 oz.
1 tablespoon fresh cilantro, chopped
1/4 teaspoon black pepper
1/4 teaspoon salt
1/4 teaspoon onion powder
Tortilla chips

Chop the jalapeños and lessen the heat by removing the seeds and ribs. (Best to wear gloves while cutting jalapeños.) In a large skillet, melt butter over medium heat. Add jalapeños, garlic, and onions to skillet. Cook for about 3 minutes or until softened.

Add tomatoes, and cook until tomatoes soften, about 3 more minutes.

Combine corn starch and evaporated milk in a medium bowl; whisk until corn starch is dissolved. Whisk in the water and add corn starch mixture to the skillet. Cook, stirring constantly, until just starting to thicken.

Add white and yellow cheese to the skillet; stir until cheese is completely melted.

Stir in green chiles, cilantro, black pepper, salt, and onion powder. Bring just to a simmer and let cook for 3 or 4 minutes.

Serve with tortilla chips. When reheating, milk or water may need to be added to thin queso.

Jalapeño Peach Dip

This creamy and delicious dip with a perfect balance of sweet and spicy will leave your taste buds craving for more.

3 packages cream cheese, softened, 8 oz. each
2/3 cup peach jam
1 can diced green chiles, 4 oz.
1 tablespoon chopped jalapeño pepper
1 cup shredded Monterey jack cheese, 4 oz.
1 cup shredded Colby cheese, 4 oz.

In a large mixing bowl, blend cream cheese, jam, chiles and jalapeño peppers until well mixed, scraping the bowl occasionally.

Spoon into a 9x9x1.5-inch dish. Sprinkle with cheese. Refrigerate. Serve with chips and/or assorted party crackers.

Yield: 15 to 20 servings.

Lone Star Guacamole Dip

Experience the flavors of Texas with this delightful Lone Star Guacamole Dip. Made with fresh ingredients and bursting with zesty goodness, this dip is a perfect accompaniment to your favorite crunchy vegetables or chips.

1 medium tomato, peeled
2 ripe avocados, peeled
4 tablespoons canned green chiles, minced
1/2 cup chopped onions
1-1/2 tablespoons white vinegar
Salt and pepper to taste

In a medium bowl. crush tomatoes and avocados. Add the rest of the ingredients. Mix well and refrigerate. Serve with carrots, celery or any vegetable or chip.

Road Kill

Serve Road Kill as a dip alongside a bag of crunchy tortilla chips. Don't let the name fool you—the combination of the creamy, cheesy, and meaty layers, combined with the crunch of the chips, creates a flavor explosion that will delight your palate.

1 lb. lean ground beef
1 medium onion, chopped
1 can refried beans, 30 oz.
1 jar taco sauce, 8 oz.
2 cups grated cheddar cheese

1 carton sour cream, 8 oz.
1 can diced green chiles, 4 oz.
1/2 cup chopped green onion tops
1 can chopped ripe olives, 4.25 oz.
Bag of tortilla chips

In a large skillet, brown beef and chopped onion. Spread refried beans in bottom of a 13x9x2-inch pan. Top with beef and onion mixture.

Spread taco sauce over beef mixture. Sprinkle with cheese. Bake in a 400 degrees F oven for about 20 minutes, until cheese melts and bubbles. Top with sour cream. Sprinkle with green chiles, green onion tops, and ripe olives. Serve as a dip with tortilla chips.

Spicy Stuffed Shells

Prepare for a fiery and flavorful delight with this recipe for Spicy Stuffed Shells. Bursting with a combination of bold ingredients, this dish is sure to make your taste buds dance with excitement.

1 lb. lean ground beef
12 jumbo pasta shells, cooked
1 jar mild picante sauce, 12 oz.
1/2 cup water
1 can tomato sauce, 8 oz.
1 can diced green chiles, 4 oz.
1 cup shredded Monterey Jack cheese
1 can crispy fried onions, 2.8 oz.

In a large skillet, brown and drain ground beef. Combine picante sauce, water, and tomato sauce; stir 1/2 cup into the meat mixture, along with the green chiles, cheese and 1/2 can crispy onions. Mix well. Fill the pasta shells with the meat mixture.

Pour the remaining sauce mixture on the bottom of a 10x10x2-inch baking dish. Top with the shells and remaining crispy fried onions. Bake at 350 degrees F for 30 minutes.

Austin Salsa

This homemade salsa recipe is packed with fresh ingredients and a perfect balance of heat and tanginess that will transport you to the heart of Texas.

8 cups tomatoes, peeled, diced, seeded
2 medium green peppers, chopped
2 jalapeño peppers, chopped
2 green onions, chopped
4 garlic cloves, chopped
3/4 cup tomato paste
1/2 cup white vinegar
2 teaspoons granulated sugar
2 teaspoons salt
1 teaspoon cayenne pepper

In a Dutch oven or large sauce pan, combine all ingredients. Bring to a boil, then simmer uncovered for about 45 minutes, stirring often, until salsa reaches desired consistency. Store in refrigerator.

Barbecued Crab Meat Taquitos

These delightful taquitos combine the sweetness of crab meat, the tanginess of barbecue sauce, and the freshness of cabbage to create a culinary experience like no other.

1 cup finely shredded cabbage
3 teaspoons finely sliced green onions
1 teaspoon mayonnaise
1 teaspoon apple cider vinegar
1 teaspoon brown sugar
1 teaspoon poppy seeds
1/2 teaspoon black pepper
1/2 teaspoon salt

3/4 cup barbecue sauce
2 cans white crab meat flaked, 6 oz. each
24 mini taco shells
1/2 cup shredded cheddar cheese

In a mixing bowl, combine cabbage, onions, mayonnaise, vinegar, brown sugar, poppy seeds, pepper, salt, and mix well then set aside.

In a small skillet, heat barbecue sauce on low heat. Add crab meat and heat thoroughly. Place mini taco shells on baking sheet and heat at 350 degrees F for 5 minutes. Spoon crab meat into shells and top each with a spoonful of cabbage mixture. Sprinkle with cheese.

Yield: 24 appetizers.

Chile Rellenos Bake

Chile Rellenos Bake is a delectable dish that combines the mild heat of poblano peppers with the richness of melted cheese. This recipe offers a twist on the classic chile rellenos.

2 cans whole green chiles, 4 oz. each (poblano peppers)
Monterey Jack cheese block, 8 oz.
4 eggs
1/3 cup milk
1/2 cup all-purpose flour
1/2 teaspoon baking powder
1/2 teaspoon salt
1/2 cup shredded cheddar cheese

Drain green chiles; halve lengthwise and remove seeds. Cut Monterey Jack cheese into strips to fit inside peppers. Wrap each pepper around a strip of Monterey Jack cheese; place in an 8x8x2-inch baking dish.

Beat eggs, add milk, and combine well; beat or whisk in flour, baking powder and salt until smooth. Pour over peppers. Sprinkle cheddar cheese on top. Bake in a moderate at 350 degrees F until golden, about 30 minutes.

Yield: 6 servings.

Swiss Onion Roll

Swiss Onion Roll is a delectable bread that combines the rich flavors of Swiss cheese, green onions, and poppy seeds. This recipe is simple to make and yields flavorful bread.

1 loaf frozen bread dough or 1 package frozen roll dough
2 cups shredded Swiss cheese
6 tablespoons butter, melted
3/4 cup finely chopped green onion
2 tablespoons poppy seeds
1/4 teaspoon salt

Let the dough thaw until pliable.

In a medium bowl, mix cheese, butter, green onion, poppy seeds, and salt.

Cut thawed loaf into 20 pieces or cut rolls in half. Arrange 1/2 dough pieces in bottom of well-greased ring mold or tube pan. Cover dough with half of the cheese mix. Top with remaining dough. Spread with remaining cheese mix. Let rise until double.

Bake at 375 degrees F for 25 to 30 minutes until golden brown and has a hollow sound.

Armadillo Eggs

These delicious bites are Armadillo Eggs, a delightful appetizer that combines the heat of jalapeño peppers with the creaminess of Monterey Jack cheese and pork sausage.

18 jalapeño peppers, whole
1/4 lb. Monterey jack cheese, cut in 1-inch strips
1 egg
1 teaspoon water
1-1/2 cups Bisquick baking mix
1 lb. pork sausage
1/2 lb. Monterey jack cheese, shredded
1 package Shake 'n Bake spicy pork or Buffalo style coating and seasoning mix

Cut a slit lengthwise into each jalapeño pepper and remove seeds and ribs. (Best to wear gloves.) Stuff peppers with strips of cheese.

In a small bowl, mix egg and water. Set aside. Knead Bisquick, pork sausage and shredded cheese until mixed well. Wrap the sausage mixture around pepper, making an egg shape. Roll in egg and water mixture then put in Shake 'n Bake bag until well coated.

Place on greased cookie sheet and bake for 25 minutes at 350 degrees F. These eggs can be sliced after baking or served whole.

Rolled Tortilla Bites

These tortilla bites are a delightful combination of creamy fillings wrapped in soft flour tortillas and served with a zesty homemade salsa.

1 package cream cheese softened, 8 oz.
1 can chopped green chiles, 4 oz.
1 jar chopped pimento, 4 oz.
1/2 cup chopped ripe olives
10 to 12 flour tortillas, (6-inch)

SALSA:
1 can diced tomatoes, 28 oz.
1/2 cup thinly sliced green onions
1 can chopped green chiles, 4 oz.
1/2 teaspoon salt
1/2 teaspoon oregano
1/2 teaspoon lemon peel
1/8 teaspoon black pepper
2 to 3 tablespoons lemon juice
2 tablespoons olive oil

Mix cream cheese, green chiles, pimento and ripe olives together. Spread a heaping tablespoonful on each tortilla. Roll tortilla and place, seam side down, on plate or tray. Chill for 2 hours.

Mix the remaining salsa ingredients together and refrigerate. When ready to serve, cut tortillas into 1-inch pieces and serve with salsa.

Breads

Hometown Grilled Cheese

Here's a delightful twist on the classic grilled cheese sandwich.

4 teaspoons butter, softened
8 slices crusty Italian bread
6 teaspoons pepper jelly
8 slices pepper jack cheese
2 links andouille sausage, grilled, each link cut into quarters and split lengthwise
8 slices muenster cheese

Spread 2 teaspoons butter on one side of four slices of bread. Spread pepper jelly on one side of the remaining slices of bread. On the slices of bread with pepper jelly, place two slices of pepper jack cheese and two pieces of grilled sausage. Cover the Andouille sausage with two slices of Muenster cheese and top with the remaining slices of bread, butter-side out.

Preheat a large skillet over medium heat. Place sandwiches, butter-side down, in the skillet and spread the remaining 2 teaspoons of butter over the tops of the sandwiches. Cook sandwiches, in batches, if necessary, for 2 to 3 minutes per side, or until golden and the cheeses are melted.

Jalapeño Pull-Apart Bread

Delight in a flavor-packed and irresistibly cheesy delight with this Jalapeño Pull-Apart Bread recipe. Packed with zesty jalapeño peppers, green onions, and a blend of three delectable cheeses, this bread is perfect for sharing and devouring.

2 cans diced jalapeño peppers, 4 oz. each
2 bunches green onions, chopped
Vegetable oil
1 cup shredded cheddar cheese
1 cup shredded Swiss cheese
2 10-count cans refrigerator biscuits
1/2 cup butter or margarine, melted
1 cup shredded Monterey jack cheese

In a large skillet, sauté jalapeño peppers and green onions in hot oil over medium heat for 5 minutes or until tender. Mix the cheddar cheese and Swiss cheese together in a bowl. Separate the biscuits and cut into quarters.

Spray a Bundt pan with nonstick cooking spray. Dip the biscuit quarters in melted butter and layer in pan alternately with the jalapeño mixture and cheese mixture, beginning and ending with a layer of biscuits. There should be 3 layers of biscuits and 2 layers of mixed cheese. Top with Monterey Jack cheese.

Bake at 350 degrees F for 30 to 35 minutes or until golden brown.

Yield: 12 servings.

Poppy Seed And Nut Filled Rolls

The combination of the tender dough, nutty or poppy seed filling, and the delicate sweetness of the confectioners' sugar makes these rolls a true delight for any occasion.

Nut Filling:

5 egg whites
3/4 cup granulated sugar
4 cups chopped nuts (walnuts or pecans)

Beat egg whites until foamy; add granulated sugar, beating well. Fold in chopped nuts. Makes enough filling for 4 nut rolls. (Canned nut filling or 1-12.5 oz. can of poppy seed filling may be used instead.)

Dough:

4 cups all-purpose flour
3/4 teaspoon baking soda
1/2 teaspoon salt
1 package dry yeast
1 cup margarine, cold
5 egg yolks
1 cup sour cream
Confectioners' sugar

In a large bowl, combine flour, baking soda, salt, and yeast. Cut in margarine until mixture resembles coarse meal. Add egg yolks and sour cream. Blend well with your hands until dough is well mixed.

Divide dough into 4 equal parts. Place each part in a bowl and wrap bowl loosely in plastic wrap; refrigerate overnight. (Dough will rise overnight.)

When dough is ready, sift confectioners' sugar on a rolling surface. Divide the 4 pieces of dough in half (this will make 8 rolls). Roll each piece of dough paper thin into a rectangle about 12 x 15 inches. Spread 1/4 of the poppy seed filling or nut filling on the dough. Starting at the long side of the rectangle, roll dough to the opposite side. Continue to roll and fill each piece of dough with the nut or poppy seed filling. Place rolls on well-greased cookie sheet.

Bake at 375 degrees F. for 20 minutes or until golden brown. Remove from oven and while still warm, sprinkle with confectioners' sugar. Slice when cool.

Side Dishes

Oven Fried Potatoes

If you're looking for a delicious side dish, these Oven Fried Potatoes are sure to please. So, gather the ingredients, preheat the oven, and get ready to be surprised with crispy, seasoned potato wedges that will impress your taste buds.

8 large, unpeeled baking potatoes, cut in wedges
1/2 cup vegetable oil
2 tablespoons grated parmesan cheese
1 teaspoon salt
1/2 teaspoon garlic powder
1/2 teaspoon paprika
1/4 teaspoon black pepper

Using 2 shallow baking dishes, arrange potato wedges in dishes, peeled side down. In a small bowl, mix oil, parmesan cheese, salt, garlic powder, paprika and black pepper. Brush over potatoes.

Bake at 375 degrees F. for 45 minutes or until potatoes are tender and golden brown, brushing occasionally with oil mixture.

Yield: 8 servings.

Hash Brown Potato Casserole

Enjoy the comforting flavors of this Hash Brown Potato Casserole. With its creamy texture, cheesy goodness, and crispy topping, this dish is sure to become a favorite at your table.

2 lbs. frozen hash browns, thawed
1 can cream of celery soup, 10.5 oz.
2 cups shredded sharp cheddar cheese
2 cups sour cream
2/3 cup chopped onions
2/3 cup margarine, melted, divided
3/4 teaspoon salt
1/4 teaspoon black pepper
2 cups crushed corn flakes

In a large bowl, mix hash browns, cheese, soup, sour cream, onions and 1/3 cup of margarine, salt, and pepper.

Spray a 3-quart casserole dish or a 13x9x2-inch baking dish with non-stick cooking spray. Pour mixture into the dish.

Mix remaining margarine with corn flakes and sprinkle over the potatoes. Bake at 350 degrees F for 40 minutes.

Yield 10 to 12 servings.

Zucchini with Salsa

Fire up the grill, gather the ingredients, and get ready to enjoy the delightful flavors of this Zucchini with Salsa recipe. Fresh zucchini slices are paired with a zesty homemade salsa, creating a delightful and healthy side dish.

4 medium zucchini, sliced
3 medium tomatoes, diced
1 medium onion, diced
3 green onions, sliced
2 jalapeño peppers, seeded and minced
2 garlic cloves, minced
1 tablespoon minced fresh cilantro
Salt and pepper to taste

Divide zucchini between two pieces of heavy-duty foil (about 20x18-inches).

In a large bowl, combine tomatoes, onion, green onions, peppers, cloves, cilantro and salt and pepper. Spoon tomato mixture over zucchini. Fold foil around vegetables and seal tightly.

Grill, covered, over indirect heat for 15 to 20 minutes or until vegetables are tender.

Yield: 10 servings.

Southern Fresh Fried Corn

Get a taste of the Southern charm with this delightful recipe for Southern Fresh Fried Corn. Made with the star ingredient of fresh corn, this dish captures the essence of summertime and is a perfect addition to any meal.

8 ears of fresh corn
2 tablespoons of bacon grease (or substitute 2 tablespoons of butter)
4 tablespoons of butter, divided
Salt and black pepper to taste

Shuck and clean the corn. One cob at a time, stand it in a large bowl and cut kernels off with a sharp knife.

Then scrape all the pulp and juice out of the cob. Just turn the knife backwards and scrape the cob gently with back of knife to get juice.

Heat a large skillet on medium heat. Melt bacon grease and 2 tablespoons of butter; add corn, salt and pepper.

Reduce heat to medium low and cook for 20 to 30 minutes, stirring frequently. Remove from heat, add remaining butter and stir until melted.

Sweet Potato Souffle

With its rich and comforting flavors, Sweet Potato Soufflé is a classic side dish that brings warmth to the table. The creamy sweet potato base, combined with the crunchy and sweet pecan topping will make any meal extra special.

3 cups mashed cooked sweet potatoes
3 eggs
1 cup granulated sugar
1/2 cup milk
1/2 cup butter or margarine
1 teaspoon vanilla extract

Combine mashed potatoes with remaining ingredients and stir to blend. Pour into a buttered 2-quart baking dish.

Topping:

1 cup brown sugar, firmly packed
1/3 cup all-purpose flour
1 cup chopped pecans
1/3 cup margarine, softened

Mix brown sugar, flour, pecans, and margarine together until crumbly. Sprinkle over potato mixture in casserole.

Bake at 400 degrees F for 30 minutes.

Yield: 8 to 10 servings.

Tomatoes Diablo

Perfect as a light appetizer or a refreshing side dish, Tomatoes Diablo will impress your taste buds with its vibrant flavors. This dish combines fresh tomatoes with a zesty dressing that adds a delightful kick of flavor.

1/2 cup sliced green onions
1/4 cup olive oil
1/4 cup vegetable oil
1/2 teaspoon freshly ground black pepper
3 tablespoons tarragon vinegar or white wine vinegar
2 teaspoons granulated sugar
2 tablespoons prepared mustard
1 teaspoon salt
7 to 8 firm ripe tomatoes peeled and sliced

Combine green onions, olive oil, vegetable oil, pepper, vinegar, sugar, mustard, and salt in a small bowl. Whisk until well blended. Place the tomato slices in a large shallow bowl or glass tray. Pour the dressing over the tomatoes.

Cover the dish with plastic wrap and let stand at room temperature for several hours. Serve at room temperature.

Texan Quicksteppers

Experience a taste of Texas with this recipe for Texan Quicksteppers. Combining the bold flavors of sharp cheddar cheese, Monterey jack cheese, and diced green chiles, these flavorful bites are sure to be a hit.

Sharp cheddar cheese, 8 oz.
Monterey jack cheese, 8 oz.
1 can diced green chiles, 4 oz.
1 egg
1 can evaporated milk, 4 oz.
Couple shakes Tabasco sauce
1 teaspoon Worcestershire sauce
1/2 teaspoon salt
1/4 teaspoon black pepper

Grate all cheese and set aside. Drain the green chiles. Cut green chiles into julienne strips (long, thin strips) and scatter evenly over the bottom of an ungreased 8x8x2-inch baking dish. Sprinkle all the cheese over the chiles.

In a small bowl, beat the egg, milk, Tabasco sauce, Worcestershire sauce, salt, and pepper, blend together. Drizzle over cheese mixture. There will not be a great deal of liquid – but don't worry – it will all blend in when it's done.

Bake at 350 degrees F. for 45 minutes or until it's set like custard. Slice into small pieces and serve hot.

Squash Fritters

These crispy and delightful Squash Fritters are made with grated butternut squash and a few pantry staples. These fritters are a perfect way to enjoy the flavors of the season.

1 small butternut squash, grated (2 cups)
1 heaping cup all-purpose flour
2 teaspoons baking powder
1/8 teaspoon salt
2 eggs
2 teaspoons granulated sugar

Mix all ingredients and drop by spoonfuls into deep fryer and fry until golden brown. Drain – roll in confectioners' sugar if desired.

Cheddar Shrimp Nachos

Packed with savory shrimp, melted cheddar cheese, and a variety of delicious toppings, these nachos are sure to be a hit at your next gathering or as a tasty snack.

3/4 lb. deveined peeled and cooked shrimp, chopped
1-1/2 cups shredded cheddar cheese
1/4 cup sliced ripe olives, drained
1 can diced roasted green chiles, drained, 4 oz.
1/3 cup green onions, chopped
1/4 teaspoon ground cumin
1/2 cup mayonnaise
45 tortilla chip scoops

In a large bowl, combine shrimp, cheddar cheese, olives, green chiles, and green onions. In a small bowl, combine cumin and mayonnaise; add to shrimp mixture and mix well.

Place tortilla chip scoops on ungreased baking sheets. Fill scoops with a tablespoon of shrimp mixture. Bake at 350 degrees F. for 5 to 10 minutes or until cheese is melted.

Once the nachos are beautifully melted and golden, remove them from the oven. Serve warm.

Yield: 4 dozen

Corn Fritter Casserole

This dish combines the sweetness of corn with creamy textures and savory ingredients, resulting in a delightful and satisfying meal.

3 teaspoons butter, softened
3 large egg whites
1 package fat-free cream cheese softened, 8 oz.
1/2 cup finely chopped onion
1/2 cup finely chopped red bell pepper
1 can whole kernel corn, drained, 15.25 oz.
1 can cream style corn, 14.75 oz.
1 package corn muffin mix, 8.5 oz.
1/4 teaspoon black pepper

In a large bowl, combine butter, egg whites and cream cheese, stirring with a whisk until smooth. Stir in onion, bell pepper, whole kernel corn, and cream style corn; mix well. Add muffin mix and black pepper, stirring until well combined.

Pour into a 9x9x2-inch baking dish coated with cooking spray. Bake at 375 degrees F. for 50 minutes or until a wooden toothpick inserted in center comes out clean.

Hot Pepper Rice

Experience a burst of flavor with every spoonful of Hot Pepper Rice. This zesty dish combines fluffy long-grain rice with tangy sour cream, diced green chiles, fresh jalapeño pepper, and a medley of cheeses.

3 cups cooked long-grain rice
1 carton sour cream, 8 oz.
1 can diced green chiles, 4 oz., drained
1 medium fresh jalapeño pepper, seeded and diced
1 8-oz. package Monterey Jack cheese, thinly sliced and divided
1/2 cup shredded Cheddar cheese

Combine the first 4 ingredients. Layer half of rice mixture in a lightly greased 10x6x2-inch baking dish, top with half of Monterey Jack cheese. Repeat procedure, sprinkle with Cheddar cheese.

Bake at 350 degrees F for 15 minutes.

Yield: 6 to 8 servings.

Cactus Country Fried Corn

With its enticing blend of fresh corn, savory bacon, and zesty onions, Cactus Country Fried Corn is a celebration of Southwestern cuisine that will add a touch of rustic charm to any meal.

6 strips bacon, cut into 1" pieces
1 medium onion, minced or in rings
4 ears corn, shucked and cleaned, kernels scraped from cob
2 small cucumbers, thinly sliced
1 large egg
1/2 teaspoon granulated sugar
1/2 teaspoon salt
1/8 teaspoon black pepper

Lightly cook bacon. Remove bacon; drain on paper towels. In a bowl, combine bacon, onion, corn, cucumbers, egg, sugar, salt, and pepper thoroughly; pour into remaining bacon drippings. Cook slowly so as not to brown too quickly, about 25 minutes.

Yield: 4 to 6 servings.

Soups And Salads

Texas Two-Step Slaw

Grab your mixing bowl and get ready to do the Texas Two-Step with this flavorful slaw. It's a dance of tastes and textures that will transport your palate to the heart of Texas.

4 cups shredded green cabbage
1 cup shredded red cabbage
1/4 cup chopped red onion
2 jalapeño peppers, seeded, finely chopped
2 tablespoons chopped fresh cilantro
1 can Mexicorn, drained, 11 oz.
1 cup shredded cheddar cheese
3/4 cup ranch salad dressing
1 tablespoon fresh lime juice
1 teaspoon cumin
Fresh cilantro sprigs

Combine green cabbage, red cabbage, red onion, jalapeño peppers, cilantro, Mexicorn and cheese in a large bowl and mix well. Combine ranch salad dressing, lime juice and cumin in a small bowl, blend well.

Pour ranch dressing mix over salad, tossing to coat. Serve immediately or refrigerate until serving time. Garnish with cilantro sprigs.

Yield: 8 servings.

Down-Home Meatball Soup

This hearty soup brings together tender meatballs, a rich tomato broth, and a blend of aromatic spices that will transport you to the heart of a down-home kitchen.

1 egg, slightly beaten
1/2 cup chopped onion
1/4 cup corn meal
1 can diced green chiles, 4 oz.
1 clove garlic, minced
3/4 teaspoon salt
1/4 teaspoon oregano
1/8 teaspoon black pepper
1 lb. ground beef
3 cups water
1 can diced tomatoes, 14.5 oz.
1 can tomato sauce, 8 oz.
1 tablespoon granulated sugar
1/2 teaspoon chili powder

In a large mixing bowl, combine egg, half of the chopped onion, corn meal, half of the green chiles, garlic, salt, oregano, pepper, and ground beef. Mix and shape into 48 meat balls. Set it aside.

In a large saucepan or Dutch oven combine water, undrained tomatoes, tomato sauce, remaining green chiles, remaining chopped onion, sugar, and chili powder. Bring mixture to a boil, stirring occasionally.

Add meatballs and bring to boil again. Cover and reduce heat; simmer for 30 minutes. Yield: 8 servings.

Taco Soup

Taco Soup is a versatile dish that can be enjoyed on its own as a filling and flavorful meal or paired with a side of warm tortillas or a fresh salad for a complete dining experience.

1 lb. lean ground beef
1/4 cup chopped onion
1 can tomatoes undrained, 14.5 oz.
1 can kidney beans undrained, 15.5 oz.
1 can whole kernel corn undrained, 15.25 oz.
1 can tomato sauce, 8 oz.
1 package taco seasoning mix, 1 oz.
Corn chips
Grated cheese
Sour cream

In a large skillet, brown ground beef and onion. Drain. In a large soup pot, add beef and onion, tomatoes, kidney beans, corn, tomato sauce and taco seasoning. Heat 20 to 30 minutes or until thoroughly heated.

Serve in bowls with corn chips, cheese, and sour cream.

Yield: 6 servings.

Gazpacho (A Cold Soup)

Gazpacho is a classic cold Spanish soup perfect for hot summer days. It is a versatile soup that can be enjoyed as a light lunch or served as an appetizer before a main course.

4 large ripe tomatoes, peeled and chopped
1 large cucumber, peeled, seeded, and diced
1 medium red onion, minced
1 green pepper, minced
1 clove garlic, minced
1 cup tomato juice
1 tablespoon red wine vinegar
3 tablespoons olive oil
Salt and pepper to taste.

In a large bowl, combine all ingredients. Blend in a blender if desired, for a smoother soup or just pulse a few times if you want the soup chunky. Chill for at least a few hours.

Spice up the soup if desired with a teaspoon of Worcestershire sauce and/or 5 drops of Tabasco sauce.

Texas Chicken Soup

With its combination of tender chicken, creamy soup, zesty salsa, and aromatic spices, Texas Chicken Soup is a comforting and flavorful dish that brings the essence of Tex-Mex cuisine to your table.

2 cups chicken broth
2 cups water
8 oz. skinned and boned chicken breast, uncooked and cut into 16 pieces
1 can cream of chicken soup, 10.5 oz.
1 cup chunky salsa (mild, medium, or hot)
1 cup hot cooked rice
1 cup frozen whole kernel corn
1/2 teaspoon dried minced garlic
1 teaspoon dried parsley flakes

In a large saucepan, combine chicken broth, water, and chicken pieces. Cook over medium heat until chicken is tender – about 10 minutes.

Stir in soup and salsa. Add rice, corn, garlic, and parsley flakes. Mix well to combine. Lower heat. Simmer for 10 minutes stirring occasionally.

Frozen Cupcake Salad

This frozen dessert combines the creamy goodness of sour cream with a medley of refreshing fruits and crunchy nuts. The result is a delightful cupcake-shaped dessert that is perfect for any occasion.

2 cups sour cream
1/8 teaspoon salt
3/4 cup granulated sugar
2 teaspoons lemon juice
1 can crushed pineapple, drained, 8 oz.
1/4 cup chopped maraschino cherries
1 banana, diced
1/4 cup chopped pecans

Blend sour cream, salt, sugar, and lemon juice together. Add pineapple, cherries, banana, and pecans. Put into paper cupcake cups that have been placed in muffin tins or cupcake pans. Freeze until ready to use. Can be made weeks ahead.

Yield: 12 servings.

Southwest Salad

Packed with wholesome ingredients and tossed in a tangy dressing, this salad is a celebration of colors, textures, and bold flavors.

1 package ready-to-serve salad greens, 9 oz.
1 can whole kernel corn, drained, 15 oz.
1 can black beans, rinsed, drained, 15 oz.
1/2 cup picante sauce
1/2 cup ranch salad dressing
1 cup broken tortilla chips
1/2 cup shredded cheddar cheese
1/2 can diced tomatoes, 14.5 oz., or fresh tomatoes

Place the greens in a large salad bowl. Top with corn and beans.

In a small bowl, mix picante sauce and ranch dressing; spoon over salad; toss to coat. Sprinkle with broken tortilla chips, cheddar cheese, and tomatoes.

Yield: 6 servings.

Black-Eyed Susan Salad

Enjoy this salad as a side dish or even as a light meal on its own. The combination of crisp black-eyed peas, sweet corn, bell peppers, and the tangy dressing creates flavors that are simply irresistible.

1 can black-eyed peas, rinsed and drained, 15 oz.
1 package frozen corn, thawed, 10 oz.
1 small green bell pepper, finely chopped
1 small red bell pepper, finely chopped
2 tablespoons finely chopped onion
1/2 cup finely chopped celery
1/4 cup cider vinegar
2 tablespoons Worcestershire sauce
1/4 cup vegetable oil
1 tablespoon granulated sugar
1/2 teaspoon garlic salt
1/8 teaspoon salt

Combine black-eyed peas, corn, bell peppers, onion, and celery in a large bowl.

In another bowl, whisk cider vinegar, Worcestershire sauce, oil, sugar, garlic salt and salt together. Pour the vinegar mixture over corn mixture and mix well. Refrigerate, covered, for 3 to 4 hours.

Yield: 6 to 8 servings.

Desserts

Black-Eyed Chew Ums

These treats combine the rich sweetness of butterscotch chips, the creamy goodness of peanut butter, the chewiness of miniature marshmallows, the fruity burst of raisins, and the crunch of corn flakes. With just a few simple steps, you can create a batch of these delightful Chew Ums that will have everyone reaching for more.

Butterscotch chips, 6 oz.
1/2 cup peanut butter
1 cup miniature marshmallows
1/2 cup raisins
1-1/2 cups corn flakes

Melt chips and peanut butter over hot water. Remove from heat and add remaining ingredients. Mix well, drop by teaspoonfuls on wax paper and chill until set.

Country Hermits

Embrace the rustic charm and inviting flavors of Country Hermits. With their simple combination of spices, molasses, raisins, and nuts, these treats are sure to become a cherished favorite in your recipe collection.

1 cup granulated sugar
1/2 cup butter or margarine
3 cups all-purpose flour
1 teaspoon baking soda
1/2 teaspoon salt
1/2 teaspoon nutmeg
1/2 teaspoon cinnamon
1/2 cup milk
1/2 cup molasses
1 cup raisins
1/2 cup chopped nuts, optional

In a large bowl, cream sugar with butter or margarine. In another bowl, sift flour with baking soda, salt, nutmeg, and cinnamon.

Mix milk and molasses. Alternately add flour mixture and milk mixture to creamed butter and sugar. Mix well. Fold in raisins, along with nuts if used.

Spread dough on greased and floured cookie sheet and bake at 350 degrees F for 20 to 25 minutes. When nearly cool, cut into squares.

Pecan Pie

This recipe for Pecan Pie combines a luscious filling made with corn syrup, eggs, butter, sugar, flour, salt, and an abundance of pecans. Each bite is a delightful combination of a flaky pie crust and a rich, caramel-like filling full of nutty pecan pieces.

1 cup light corn syrup (Karo)
3 eggs - slightly beaten
1/4 cup butter
1/2 cup sugar
3 tablespoons all-purpose flour
1/2 teaspoon salt
1 cup pecans, broken
1 pie crust shell

In a medium bowl, mix corn syrup, eggs, and butter. In another bowl, combine sugar, flour, and salt. Add sugar mixture to egg mixture; mix well. Stir in broken pecan pieces.

Pour into pie shell. Bake for one hour at 350 degrees F.

Cowboy Cookies

Packed with an array of mix-ins such as oats, dates, raisins, pecans, and chocolate chips, each bite of these Cowboy Cookies offers a combination of flavors. Get ready to enjoy a batch of these delicious cookies that capture the spirit of the Wild West.

1-1/2 cups all-purpose flour
1/2 cup whole wheat flour
1/2 teaspoon baking powder
1/2 teaspoon salt
1 cup vegetable oil
1 cup brown sugar, packed
1 cup granulated sugar
2 eggs
1 teaspoon vanilla extract
2 cups quick-cooking oats
3/4 cup chopped dates
1/2 cup chopped raisins
1/2 cup chopped pecans
3/4 cup chocolate chips

Optional additions:
Coconut
Chopped dried apricots
Chopped walnuts
Butterscotch chips

In a medium bowl, combine all-purpose flour and whole wheat flour, baking powder and salt.

In a large bowl, cream vegetable oil, brown sugar, and granulated sugar; blend in eggs and vanilla. Beat well. Add flour mixture and mix well. Add oats, dates, raisins, pecans, and chocolate chips; mix thoroughly. The dough will be crumbly. Drop by teaspoonfuls onto greased cookie sheets, using fingers to shape together. Bake at 350 degrees F. for about 12 minutes, or until golden. Remove to rack to cool. Yield: about 6 dozen.

Quick Filled Muffins

Quick Filled Muffins are a delightful treat for breakfast, brunch, or as an anytime snack. They have a surprise filling of sweet jam and nuts. Whether enjoyed warm or at room temperature, these muffins are sure to bring a smile to your face.

1-2/3 cups all-purpose flour
2 teaspoons baking powder
2/3 cup granulated sugar
1 teaspoon salt
1 egg, beaten
1/3 cup vegetable oil
2/3 cup milk
1/3 cup drained crushed pineapple
2/3 cup jam
3 tablespoons nuts chopped

Sift together flour, baking powder, sugar, and salt; make a well in the center. Add egg, oil, milk, and pineapple; mix until flour is moistened.

Fill well-greased large muffin cups half full. In a small bowl, combine jam and nuts.

Place a teaspoon on top of each muffin. Bake at 400 degrees F for 25 minutes. Remove from pan immediately.

Texas Dirt Cake

Enjoy a taste of Texas with this irresistible dessert known as Texas Dirt Cake. This rich and creamy treat is a delightful combination of chocolate sandwich cookies, creamy filling, and a velvety pudding layer.

1 package of chocolate sandwich cookies, 20 oz.
1/2 cup butter, softened
1 package fat free cream cheese, 8 oz. softened
1 cup confectioners' sugar
1 carton fat free frozen whipped topping, 12 oz., thawed
1 package instant vanilla pudding, 3.4 oz.
3 cups skim milk
1 teaspoon vanilla

Crush cookies to fine crumbs and layer half of the crumbs in a 13x9x2-inch baking dish.

With electric mixer, beat together butter and cream cheese until smooth. Add confectioners' sugar and beat well. Fold in whipped topping.

In another bowl, mix pudding, milk and vanilla; whisk until smooth and slightly thickened. Combine cream cheese mixture and pudding mixture, folding until well combined. Pour pudding mixture over crumbs in pan. Sprinkle with remaining crumbs.

Chill until ready to serve.

Yield: 20 servings.

Jell-O Cut Out Cookies

Add a burst of color and fruity flavor to your cookie jar with these delightful Jell-O Cut Out Cookies. Made with a handful of simple ingredients, these cookies are as fun to make as they are to eat.

1-1/2 cups butter
1 cup granulated sugar
1 package Jell-O gelatin dessert mix, any flavor, 3 oz.
1 egg
1 teaspoon vanilla
4 cups all-purpose flour
1 teaspoon baking powder

Cream butter, sugar, Jell-O, egg, and vanilla together. Add flour a little at a time, then add baking powder. Chill in refrigerator for about 30 minutes.

Roll out dough to 1/4-inch thickness and cut out the cookies. Use cookie cutters of your choice to create fun and festive shapes.

Bake at 350 degrees F for about 13 minutes.

Yield: about 4 dozen.

Use various Jell-O flavors and seasonal cookie cutters, if desired. For example, strawberry and lime Jell-O can be used to make red and green cookies for Christmas. Enjoy on their own or decorate with icing and sprinkles.

Good-N-Ugly Cake

This charmingly named dessert defies its unconventional appearance with an explosion of flavor. Each slice is a delightful surprise, with a blend of buttery cake and creamy icing on the bottom.

1 cup margarine, melted, divided
1/2 cup nuts
1 package butter cake mix
1 package cream cheese, softened, 8 oz.
1 box confectioners' sugar, 1 lb.

Pour 1/2 cup of melted margarine in a 13x9x2-inch pan. Sprinkle with nuts. Prepare the butter cake mix as directed on package. Pour batter over margarine and nuts.

In a large bowl, add the remaining 1/2 cup margarine. Mix in cream cheese. Add confectioners' sugar and beat with a mixer until smooth.

Spoon cream cheese mixture over cake batter and bake at 275 degrees F for about 55 minutes. When done, the icing will go to the bottom of the pan.

Yield: 24 servings.

Tex-Mex Fruit Cake

The Tex-Mex Fruit Cake is a delightful twist on the traditional fruit cake with a touch of Southwestern flair.

2 cups all-purpose flour
1 cup granulated sugar
2 teaspoons baking soda
1 can crushed pineapple undrained, 20 oz.
2 eggs, beaten
1 cup nuts
1 cup raisins

Frosting:

1 package cream cheese, 8 oz.
1/2 cup margarine, softened
2 teaspoons vanilla
2 cups confectioners' sugar

Mix flour, sugar, baking soda and pineapple. Add eggs, chopped nuts and raisins.

Bake in a greased and floured 13x9x2-inch pan for 30 to 40 minutes at 350 degrees F.

Mix frosting and spread on cake.

Southwest Bread Pudding

This Southwest Bread Pudding is a versatile dessert that can be enjoyed on its own or served with a dollop of whipped cream or a drizzle of caramel sauce for an extra touch.

1/2 medium apple
1 banana
1/4 cup walnuts
1/2 cup raisins
8 slices day old French bread
3 tablespoons melted butter
1/2 cup Monterey Jack cheese (optional)
2 cups milk
4 eggs, beaten
3/4 cup granulated sugar
1 teaspoon vanilla
1 teaspoon ground cinnamon

Chop apple and banana into a large bowl; add walnuts and raisins.

Tear bread into pieces and place in an 8x8x2-inch baking dish. Drizzle butter over bread. Sprinkle fruit and nuts mixture over bread. Sprinkle cheese over fruit and nuts.

In a medium mixing bowl, combine milk, eggs, sugar, vanilla, and cinnamon. Pour milk mixture over all in the baking dish. Lightly push down on bread mixture until all the bread is covered in the milk mixture.

Place in oven at 350 degrees F. for 45 minutes. The top will be golden brown.

Chocolate Zucchini Cake

This Chocolate Zucchini Cake recipe combines the richness of chocolate and the moistness of zucchini to create a treat that will satisfy any sweet tooth.

1/2 cup butter, softened
1/2 cup vegetable oil
1-3/4 cups of granulated sugar
1 teaspoon vanilla
2 eggs
1/2 cup of buttermilk

1/2 cup of cocoa powder
1/2 teaspoon baking powder
1 teaspoon baking soda
1 teaspoon salt
2-1/2 cups all-purpose flour

2 cups coarsely grated zucchini
1/2 cup chocolate chips
1/2 cup chopped nuts

In a large bowl, cream butter, oil, and sugar. Blend in vanilla, eggs, and buttermilk. Stir in cocoa powder, baking powder, baking soda, salt, flour, and zucchini.

Pour into a greased and floured 13x9x2-inch baking dish. Top with chocolate chips and nuts. Bake at 325 degrees F for about 50 minutes.

Bronco Brownies

These Bronco Brownies are perfect for any occasion. The recipe combines the rich flavors of caramel, chocolate, and nuts to create a delicious dessert.

1 bag caramels about 50, 14 oz.
2/3 cup evaporated milk
1 box German chocolate cake mix, 15.25 oz.
3/4 cup margarine, melted
3/4 cup chopped walnuts, optional
1 cup chocolate chips

In a medium saucepan, melt caramels with 1/3 cup of evaporated milk; set aside.

Combine cake mix, 1/3 cup evaporated milk, and melted margarine; mix well and add nuts. Press half the dough into a greased 13x9x2-inch baking dish.

Bake 5 to 10 minutes at 350 degrees F. Remove from oven and sprinkle with the chocolate chips. Pour the melted caramel milk over the chocolate chips.

Top with remaining dough and try to it spread evenly. Bake 20 minutes more at 350 degrees F.

Texas Yum Yum Cake

This yummy dessert features layers of buttery pecan crust, cream cheese and Cool Whip filling, vanilla, and chocolate pudding.

1 cup softened butter or margarine
1 cup all-purpose flour
1 cup chopped pecans
Softened cream cheese, 8 oz.
1 cup confectioners' sugar
1 carton Cool Whip, 8 oz.
1 package vanilla instant pudding mix, 3.4 oz.
4 cups cold milk
1 package chocolate instant pudding mix, 3.9 oz.
1 square semi-sweet chocolate grated, 1 oz.

Cream softened butter and flour. Add chopped pecans. Spread to all sides and even out in a 13x9x2-inch baking dish. Bake at 350 degrees F. for 20 minutes. Let cool for 30 minutes.

Cream softened cream cheese with confectioners' sugar. Fold in Cool Whip. Spread 1 cup of Cool Whip mixture over cooled crust. Put in refrigerator for 30 minutes.

Mix instant vanilla pudding with 2 cups cold milk; spread over Cool Whip mixture. Put in refrigerator for 20 minutes.

Mix instant chocolate pudding with the remaining 2 cups of milk; spread over vanilla pudding. Let set in refrigerator for 20 minutes.
Top with remaining Cool Whip mixture. Sprinkle with chopped pecans and grated chocolate.

Happiness Filled Cupcakes

Savor the moment as you bite into this moist cake and discover the creamy surprise inside. These moist and chocolatey treats are sure to bring a smile to your face and brighten your day.

3 cups all-purpose flour
2 cups granulated sugar
1/2 cup cocoa powder
2/3 cup vegetable oil
2 teaspoons baking soda
2 cups water
2 teaspoons vinegar
2 teaspoons vanilla

Filling:

Cream cheese, 8 oz., softened
1 egg
2/3 cup granulated sugar
1/4 teaspoon salt
1/2 cup coconut, optional
3/4 cup chocolate chips

Mix the filling ingredients together and set aside. In a large bowl, combine the remaining ingredients together until mixed thoroughly. Line a cupcake pan with paper liners. Fill each liner about 1/2 full. (The batter will be very thin and almost like water – that is the way it should appear.)

Place a heaping teaspoon of filling in the middle of each cupcake. Bake 25 to 30 minutes at 350 degrees F.

Texas Sheet Cake

This delectable Texas Sheet Cake is a true Texan gem that boasts a tender and moist texture, combined with a rich chocolate flavor.

Cake

1/2 cup butter or margarine
1 cup water
1/2 cup vegetable oil
4 teaspoons cocoa powder
2 cups all-purpose flour
2 cups granulated sugar
1/2 teaspoon salt
1/2 cup buttermilk
1 teaspoon baking soda
1 egg
1 teaspoon vanilla

Grease a 10x15-inch cookie sheet (with edges) or bar pan.

In a large saucepan, combine butter, water, oil, and cocoa. Bring to a boil and then cool slightly. Add flour, granulated sugar, and salt. Mix well until smooth. Add buttermilk, baking soda, egg and vanilla. Mix until smooth and glossy.

Pour into prepared pan and bake at 400 degrees F. for 15 to 18 minutes or until center is set. Pour frosting over warm bars. Cool.

Sheet Cake Frosting

1/4 cup butter
6 teaspoons milk
4 teaspoons cocoa powder
1 teaspoon vanilla
2 cups confectioners' sugar

In large saucepan, combine butter, milk, and cocoa powder. Bring to a boil and remove from heat. Stir in confectioners' sugar and vanilla, mixing until smooth.

Other Books by Southern Soup Jockeys:

Favorite Cake Mix Recipes

100 Favorite Squash Recipes

The Best Texas Cookbook – 100 Favorite Lone Star Recipes

Made in the USA
Coppell, TX
07 July 2023

18821314R00079